ACCLA

Doretha Dingler

"Mary Kay founded her Company emphasizing priorities of God first, family second, and career third. Those priorities catapulted Doretha Dingler to the top of the Mary Kay sales force. After I met Mary Kay Ash in 1968, and was asked to travel the nation to speak to her sales force, I worked with Doretha when she helped teach those Mary Kay priorities in the Company's early days. You'll love the story of this influential Mary Kay pioneer."

—ZIG ZIGLAR, BESTSELLING AUTHOR AND MOTIVATIONAL SPEAKER

"One of the reasons I've been successful is that I paid close attention to what Doretha Dingler did with her Mary Kay business and what she showed me about leadership. Here is a principled woman who defines the classic role of a mentor. Doretha has been a guiding force in the lives of so many women like me who were lacking in confidence until shown how to tap into their inner strength, how to soar. I also know how much Mary Kay Ash trusted her and how proud she would be to have you read this book."

—BARBARA SUNDEN, MARY KAY'S CURRENT NO. 1
ELITE EXECUTIVE INDEPENDENT NATIONAL SALES DIRECTOR,
EARNING OVER $1 MILLION PER YEAR EVERY YEAR SINCE 2008

"As the physician who has treated the Dingler family for the last twenty-five years, it has been a heartening journey for me to watch Doretha in action—overcoming obstacles and always maintaining a determined attitude. She went to the top in a very competitive industry when all the odds were stacked against her. I cite her example many times to patients who want to give up when faced with medical challenges. I recommend this book and will personally share it with colleagues, friends, and patients."

—DR. CASEY CALDWELL, THE MAYO CLINIC

"One of my favorite memories was when I studied Advanced Economics in my junior year of high school. In our textbook, a chapter on 'Leading Entrepreneurs' featured Mary Kay Ash. I realized what it was that my Dee Dee had done. I knew she was one of the first to help Mary Kay be a frontrunner in the business world."

—BRITTANY JORDAN DINGLER, GRANDDAUGHTER

In Pink

The Personal Story of a Mary Kay
Pioneer Who Made History Shaping
a New Path to Success for Women

Doretha Dingler

Published by:

 Brevin, LLC
Scottsdale, Arizona

ISBN-13: 978-0-9853725-1-4

Cover design by Gary A. Rosenberg
Produced by The Book Couple • www.thebookcouple.com

Printed in the United States of America

Dedicated to my beautiful granddaughter,
Brittany Jordan Dingler.

The mutual unconditional love we have for each
other inspired me to share my story not only
with her, but also with my Mary Kay family,
keeping Mary Kay's legacy alive from
someone who knows firsthand her
invaluable contribution to the
status of women.

Contents

Overview

There is no better way to appreciate the legend of Mary Kay than to view it through the eyes of a woman who started a Mary Kay business in the early days of the famed cosmetics company. This is the story of Doretha Dingler, who by following her mentor's lead worked her way to the very top of the Independent sales force against all odds.

Following Doretha's amazing journey is a great lesson in understanding why the Wharton School of Business has hailed Mary Kay Ash as one of the great leaders of our time and how her company has come to be known as "an opportunity generating machine" in a Harvard Business School case study. Doretha is one of only a handful of women in Mary Kay history who have achieved the No. 1 ranking, and because her journey takes place in the half-century that forever changed the trajectory of women, it's filled with compelling lessons for women today.

This memoir is a fitting commemoration of the tenth year since Mary Kay's death, written by the woman who reigned as the No. 1 Independent National Sales Director when Mary Kay died in 2001. As the storied Mary Kay Company approaches its fiftieth anniversary in 2013, here is a story that celebrates the ideals that Mary Kay Ash built her empire on, a fitting testament to just how far belief and an opportunity can carry an ordinary woman.

—Yvonne Pendleton

During her nearly twenty years at Mary Kay Inc., Yvonne was director of corporate heritage, academic outreach, and executive speechwriting. She worked closely with Mary Kay Ash and was with her in her office the day Mary Kay first fell ill and subsequently suffered the stroke that would rob her of her voice. In addition to writing for and with Mary Kay Ash, she worked with Executive Chairman Richard Rogers upon his return to the Company in 2000, as well as Mary Kay's grandson and current company executive, Ryan Rogers. During her tenure, Yvonne wrote for every chief executive and every president in the history of Mary Kay Inc., including those who hold the titles now. Yvonne's contribution to *In Pink* has been equally invaluable.

United States

Canada

DINGLER

Brazil

Philippines

AREA

Mexico

Korea

#1 WORLDWIDE

Czech Republic

2003

England

At the time of her retirement, Doretha's area was represented in all 50 states and multiple countries. She was one of only five Independent National Sales Directors to have ever held the title of #1 Worldwide in the 40-year history of Mary Kay, Inc.

Preface

In Pink is a story that wasn't originally meant to be shared with the world. It was about a desire to create the story of my journey as a wife, mother and grandmother, complete with pictures and stories (in scrapbook form) for my granddaughter, Brittany . . . and in the process discovered that an incredible Mary Kay success story was being revealed, a story that had to be told.

It's a story I've told in one version or another so many times and in so many venues throughout my nearly forty-year career with Mary Kay Inc. that you'd think even I would be tired of it by now. But old habits die hard, and I think I still have a few nuggets of value to share, especially from the comfortable vantage point of retirement, with it's perfect twenty-twenty hindsight. And so once more, with feeling, here is the travelogue of my incredible journey—complete with shortcuts and travel advisories—to help the intrepid traveler find her way.

One of the unique aspects of the Mary Kay sales force is that, unlike most other companies, there is no such thing as a "lateral hire." No one has ever started as a Director or a National Sales Director because she was a rainmaker at some other company. We all started as consultants with the same beauty case and the same unlimited opportunity. Those who rose did so by listening, really listening, to the "I Stories" of those beside them, those above them, and to Mary Kay herself. An "I Story" is one of the many ingenius methods Mary Kay Ash developed to help us teach and motivate one another. We all need someone or something to give us our own "I can do it" moment to keep us moving forward.

And so, just as I learned from and was inspired by all those women who shared their stories with me, I feel excited to share my story with you, because if there is some woman in rural East Texas or Bejing China who can identify with, and be encouraged by my story, then the decision to parlay a personal scrapbook into a world-wide success story will have been worth it! This is indeed a must-read to learn a tried and proven formula for success! If I can do this, so can you!!

—Doretha Dingler

1

If I Can Do This, So Can You

"If you can dream it, you can do it."
—WALT DISNEY

I was trapped. Trapped with no way out except the one direction I could not, did not want to go—onto the stage. And then to the podium where I would have to turn and face a room full of my fellow Independent Sales Directors for the first and last speech of my soon-to-be-over Mary Kay career. When Mary Kay sent me the special delivery letter asking me to give this speech, to talk about how I had gone from the brink of termination to Director in six months, I tried everything to get out of it. I felt a bit like Moses who, after being commanded by God to speak to Pharaoh, begged God to let his brother Aaron speak for him because Aaron was such an eloquent speaker whereas Moses felt he himself was "slow of speech and tongue." I even had an Aaron, so to speak, a confident and eloquent speaker in my Unit whom I suggested to Mary Kay as a substitute that I was certain would do a far better job than I ever could, but Mary Kay was never one to let people give into their fears and would have none of it.

To make matters worse, my husband sided with Mary Kay. Instead of helping me fake my death like a truly supportive spouse, he took a week off from his job, arranged for his mother to take care of our then three-year-old son, Devin, and then drove me to Dallas from Greenville, South Carolina, so I could make this one-hour (!) speech. The one ingenious thing he did say to keep me going, however, was that I could quit the company and avoid any further speaking engagements for the rest of my life as soon as I gave this one speech. One and done. That was my plan.

AIRMAIL SPECIAL DELIVERY

If at all possible, I would like to reserve an hour on June 12 for you to talk to the Directors at the Directors' meeting telling them some of your "Secrets of Success." Would you please let me know if you can make this Directors' meeting?

Mary Kay, Chairman of the Board

Excerpt from letter to me from Mary Kay in June of '69
asking me to make a ONE HOUR speech.

Well, of course the conspiracy worked. I somehow survived the speech, and when Mary Kay congratulated me later and told me she was proud of me, I decided to put off my resignation just a bit longer. Besides, I had learned that only the top ten Directors were asked to speak at the annual Mary Kay Seminar—my ultimate fear—so all I had to do was stay off that dreaded list and I was home free. No more speeches for yours truly. Of course, as usual, God had other plans.

Almost forty years and well over a hundred speeches later, I faced another audience. It was my retirement speech presented to the attendees of Leadership Conference in Long Beach, California, and I can't recall a single but-

terfly as I took the stage for the last time. By now I had pretty much forgiven Mary Kay and Bruce for that day in Dallas so many years ago and, as always, they were right. It wasn't so much that I learned to speak in front of an audi-

With Bruce's mother

ence, it was that I learned I could overcome even my worst fear. I also came to learn that I could help other people face their fears (and thereby begin to discover their own potential) and that the more of us there were, the easier it became.

I had had some experience in the corporate world prior to join-ing Mary Kay, and it was my experience that in other companies people tried their best to hide their fears. Employees tried to act like they had arrived as fully formed selling, leading, public-speaking machines just waiting for someone else to stumble so they could advance. In Mary Kay, however, it was, as my granddaughter used to say, "opposite day." We admitted our fears and insecurities to one another so that we could then explain how we overcame them. Mary Kay

> I learned I could overcome even my worst fear.

understood that it was far easier for a woman to overcome her fears when another woman was standing on the step just above her saying, "It's okay. I was in your shoes, and if I can do it, so can you . . . just follow me."

As with so many other things, Mary Kay was right on target. She taught us to lead by example, and we soon learned that not only was it good for the bottom line, it was good for us. The positive feeling one gets when closing a sale or signing up a new recruit pales in comparison to the feeling of seeing the lightbulb go off in a woman's eyes when she realizes "I can really do this," then watching her grow into the successful, confident woman she was always meant to be. It is an addictive feeling and the foundation of the Mary Kay experience. We only do well by doing good so that when

we are recognized—and anyone who's ever been to a Mary Kay Seminar knows Mary Kay pulls out all the stops when it comes to recognition—we can feel good that we didn't take from someone else, we simply gave and it was given back to us. I like to think that we didn't actually need handrails to reach the Mary Kay stage because

> I hadn't the slightest notion I was about to become part of a "movement," and one among the first real wave of American career women.

one hand was always reaching up to the woman ahead of us and the other reaching down to the woman below until we all stood together, arm in arm, enjoying one another's success.

When Mary Kay launched her "dream company" in 1963, women didn't really have any professional role models in business, and many times over the years I've wondered how Mary Kay Ash could possibly have known that so many women just like me were waiting for the chance to do something more with our lives, even if we didn't quite know what that "something" was. In fact, I wouldn't have been the least bit curious about Mary Kay if my plans to start a family as soon as we were settled in our first home with my husband's first post-college job had materialized. Instead, with all the boxes checked except "start a family," I filled my days with church activities, volunteering at the YMCA, cooking clubs, bowling, three bridge clubs, and my Beta Sigma Phi sorority. And yet, despite all of that activity I still felt restless, so I kept searching for that elusive something that still seemed to be missing.

Doretha Dingler
ΒΣΦ

Well, to say the least, my search soon came to an end, though at the time it certainly didn't look like destiny. It looked like a wig party with a few skin care products that had been mixed up in the lids of fruit jars. *Hardly the stuff dreams are made of.* Of course, you have to remember that at the time there weren't many "career women" out there, certainly not in East Texas anyway, and most women, myself included, were just looking for an opportunity to socialize and maybe earn a little extra spending money. Believe me when I tell you that I hadn't the slightest notion I was about to become part of a "movement," and one among the first real wave of American career women.

... it certainly didn't look like destiny. It looked like a wig party with a few skin care products that had been mixed up in the lids of fruit jars.

I still remember the day during my senior year of high school when my friend's mother offered to drive some of us girls the seventy-five miles from Athens, Texas, where I was born and raised, into Dallas so we could look for jobs that (hopefully) would be waiting for us after graduation. I jumped at the chance. I didn't dare tell my parents we were going (we actually played hooky from school that day). I knew they felt that eighteen years old was way too young to move to the big city, especially for a girl. In Dallas, the three of us went to one company we'd heard was hiring, the Trader's and General Insurance Company, to put in our applications. Although I had fully intended to apply for an entry-level position (which was log-ical since I hadn't even graduated high school yet), I soon found myself handing in an application for secretary to a senior executive. To my mind, as the position had recently become available, I thought it couldn't hurt to try. I loved taking shorthand and typing (in fact, had repre-sented my school in district competi-tion), was office assistant for our high school principal, had an eye for detail, and had rare work experience from going to work with my dad since I was nine years old. Well, to my amazement, I got the job and it set my course for the future.

> Too often today, people are acutely aware of what they can't do and are not empowered to find out what they can do.

If I were pressed to say why I applied for that first job that seemed so clearly beyond my qualifications, I'd have to say that it was mostly because I didn't know any better. My granddaughter, Brittany, is growing up in a world where so much information is available at the push of a button (on her phone, no less!), and while I think having more information is usually a good thing, there are times that too much information can be a detriment. Too often today, people are acutely aware of what they can't do and are not empowered to find out what they can do. I, for one, am glad I was-n't able to Google that position on my smart phone and find out what the odds were of an eighteen-year-old not-yet-high-school-graduate being hired as secretary to a senior executive of a major insurance company. All I knew was that I liked to be challenged with my work and wanted to get the best job I could find. Well, with that job waiting for me after graduation, I didn't even consider accepting the scholarships offered me from Draughn Business College or Mary Hardin–Baylor College (much to the disappointment of my high school principal, Mr. Fluker).

Of course I didn't consider for a moment that I was embarking on a "career," I had merely found a challenging way to support myself until I found Mr. Right. Once he showed up, I could put all of this business about business behind me and focus on raising a family, right? Well, as usual, life didn't turn out the way I had planned, and that annoying tendency of mine to act first and calculate the odds of success later would turn out to be a tremendous asset when destiny (and Mr. Right) finally caught up with me.

Much has been written about the feminist movement of the 1960s and how it was supposedly rooted in the discontent of housewives. I remember they called it "the problem that has no name." The pioneers of Mary Kay were not feminists but, for the most part, reasonably happy housewives with a desire to explore another side of themselves. Mary Kay took great pains to distance herself and her company from any kind of label or rhetoric, saying she found it much more effective to simply equip women with the tools and business skills they would need "once they had a track to run on." She believed we were up to any challenge, and, as I've said many times, she believed in us a long time before most of us believed in ourselves. Mary Kay, of course, created that "track" in the

> . . . find your confidence . . . get out of your comfort zone, overcome your fears, and begin the journey.

form of a company with a unique and unlimited opportunity for women. But, as we soon learned, before we could lace up our sneakers and really run, we had to address many of the issues that were holding us back even though we may not have realized them at the time.

If I had only one message to impart that might help you be successful, it would be simply to start. To find your confidence, get out of your comfort zone, overcome your fears, and begin the journey to discover and accomplish what you want to do with your life. Mary Kay will not be the totality of every woman's journey. For some, it may be just the beginning, a launching pad for some other aspiration. For others, it may be a place to step out of the rat race and find their own pace, or perhaps merely serve as inspiration, proof that every woman has the right to realize her own potential. No matter your particular dream or ultimate path in life, it is a comfort to know that there is always a place where it's okay to be a confident, successful woman and where there will always be other like-minded women just waiting to inspire you to take that leap of faith and become who you were always meant to be.

> . . . every woman has the right to realize her own potential.

I can recall a 2001 speech in which I quoted the female chair of the Federal Reserve of Boston who said, "For all the real progress women have made in education, in their choice of career, and in their pay, a relatively small percentage ever make it to the top. Studies suggest, and my own experience has confirmed, that it is hard for women to believe they can progress if they cannot look up and see faces like their own at the top." While I have been flattered

With my cousin Lois, who joined Mary Kay and became a Director.

over the years by the many women who have asked to hear my story, the idea that other women might look up to me or be inspired by my success has always come to me as a bit of a shock. Honestly, because the Mary Kay business model is to grow by helping others succeed, I was so focused on the goals of my Unit and later my Area that I often wasn't even aware I'd crossed another threshold of achievement until I heard it from someone else. I once shared this with Mary Kay, and she told me that's exactly how it was for her. She didn't have dollar signs in her eyes, but when she looked up, there they were.

Mary Kay began her company on a very simple premise: Create an opportunity that will allow women to reach their true potential on their own terms and you can't help but succeed. It was highly unusual for women of her era, but out of necessity Mary Kay had worked her entire life. Over twenty-five years, she developed this great dream that was centered on her belief in the potential of women. It came out of what she'd seen women endure in the working world, and it was shaped purely out of her belief in what women could achieve given the right opportunity. Though she initially had intended to share her wisdom and experience with other women by writing a book (no small task, I can assure you), Mary Kay ultimately decided to apply her vast knowledge of sales and business to creating a company that would provide a unique opportunity for all those women she knew were out there (and the many more who would come later) to realize their strength, their beauty, and their worth.

> Over twenty-five years, she developed this great dream that was centered on her belief in the potential of women.

As I said in the preface, this is my "I story." My "If I can do this so can you" story that I share, not to brag about my accomplishments, but in the hopes that if there is some young woman in rural East Texas (or even rural Estonia these days) who can identify with and be encouraged by my story, then it will be there for her. The women who inspired me along the way may not have inspired all of my peers but, as the company grew, we all seemed to find someone who gave us our own "I can do it" moment and kept us moving forward . . . even when our shoes were killing us!

With my mentors Mary Kay
and Helen McVoy

2

The "Wig Party" That Changed My Life

"Experience is something you get looking for something else."
—MARY PETTIBONE POOLE

*B*eing invited to a social event with some of my friends was the kind of outing I really looked forward to, so I didn't consider my girlfriend's invitation to a wig party as anything other than a chance to get out of the house. I had no inkling that I might find my life's calling at this event; I simply wanted to try on the wigs. I didn't even know that the event included cosmetics! For those of you still scratching your heads, back in the early days Mary Kay had a line of Fashion Tress wigs as a lead-in to introduce her new

Out on the town with our good friends the Colliers and the Weems in Dallas

skin care products because in the sixties wigs were quite an attention getter, and Mary Kay prudently took advantage of their popularity to build her business.

Meanwhile, back at the wig party, my girlfriends Hilda, Pam, and I were more than fashionably late. In fact, we were told by the Consultant hosting the party that we were too late to try on the wigs and that there wouldn't even be enough time for us to sample any of the cosmetics or skin care products. I remember feeling humiliated by this rejection, but when the consultant suggested we could come to another event, I decided to try again. This time, I did arrive on time, and I did buy the basic skin care set for $15.95 (I never did buy a wig). It contained those five basic products that spawned the Mary Kay cosmetics empire: cleanser, skin freshener, moisturizer, night cream, and a foundation makeup. A truism about women is that when we find something we like, our first instinct is to tell everyone about it. I got so enthused about this great line of products I'd discovered at the wig party that I did just that—told everyone I knew about it. Someone said if I loved it so much, maybe I should consider selling it. On the strength of that statement, I made a life-changing decision and became a Mary Kay beauty consultant. Bruce was just getting started in his engineering career, however, and I didn't want to do anything to conflict with that, but he assured me it wouldn't be a problem and that his support was there for me 100 percent.

> A truism about women is that when we find something we like, our first instinct is to tell everyone about it.

Now, just in case some of you think I only joined Mary Kay for the glamour (and the wigs), let me describe a typical class/party as it was conducted in 1965. First, those of you accustomed to having individually sterilized and hermetically sealed product trays designed to be used once and then disposed of will be shocked to learn that we recycled the same trays for use in every class. The instructions we were given to maintain proper hygiene said to clean the trays with alcohol after each use and then place them in the oven for sixty seconds at 140 degrees until they glazed slightly. What happened if you left them in longer than that? Well, then you could dispose of them. And if more people showed up for a class than you had trays for? No problem. Fruit jar lids made an excellent back-up palette for mixing product, and in those days we all had them in abundance. I can hear you out there snickering at the image of us wearing wigs and mixing product in fruit jar lids, but we had a lot of fun and sold a lot of product, and though styles (and regulatory standards) may have changed, it's still fundamentally about a great product providing a great opportunity for women everywhere. And *that* will never go out of style.

> It's still fundamentally about a great product providing a great opportunity for women everywhere.

No sooner had I signed on the dotted line, however, than I came down with what I thought was a strange illness that turned out to be a fairly common malady. I was pregnant. Bruce and I had wanted children since college, and I had even gone into Dallas with a friend who was seeing a fertility specialist and suggested I do the same. After six painful but seemingly unsuccessful treatments, however, I suppose I had just given up on the possibility of starting a family, and then, nine months after starting my Mary Kay business, our only child Devin was born. We were, of course, ecstatic to have a seemingly healthy baby boy (ten fingers, ten toes, etc.), but then something wholly unexpected happened. Just as I was starting to wonder why I appeared to be the only new mother who had not had her baby brought to her, a pediatrician I hadn't even met before came into my room with a very somber expression and explained to me that my baby was blue and that, in his opinion,

Devin had a major heart valve problem and would probably not live beyond his fifth birthday (and only then if several subsequent surgeries were successful). We later learned that Dr. Jim Nicholson, a very prominent physician who delivered Devin, was furious that the pediatrician had not used more professional judgment in delivering this news to a new mother, especially in light of the fact that I had no one to help me process this awful news since

Six months pregnant at home with Bruce and Prince.

Bruce had briefly gone back to the office to take care of a few things before Devin was discharged.

Due to the fact that I was sobbing uncontrollably, it took three attempts before I was able to reach Bruce at the office. Every time I dialed the phone and the secretary answered, I broke down and had to hang up. Finally, after the third attempt, I managed to control my emotions enough to get him on the phone. Of course, he was back at the hospital immediately and as upset as I was, but he was more focused on taking care of me since Devin was in good hands with a team of doctors and nurses looking after him and I seemed to be the one deteriorating. Bruce did everything in his power to soothe my frazzled nerves and keep me calm (no small task, I can assure you) while we waited for the official diagnosis. Fortunately,

Finally bringing Devin home from the hospital.

within two days (two very long, prayer-filled days) Devin had his color back and was pronounced perfectly healthy. Another miracle.

As we later learned, Devin's condition wasn't that unusual and, most of the time, as in Devin's case, it corrects itself. Unfortunately, since the pediatrician had only seen this condition one other time, and that baby did in fact have the heart problem he had described, Devin was kept in the hospital an extra week for observation (and if Bruce hadn't held his temper in check, they would have had to keep the pediatrician in the hospital for observation). Well, it should come as no surprise that for the next eighteen months after that harrowing experience I spent every waking hour staring at Devin. And he stared back at me.

Devin and me, staring at each other.

As for my still like-new Mary Kay beauty case, it had been decisively kicked under the crib where it lay all but forgotten (I did manage to place a few orders for my neglected customers here and there) as I commenced living the life I had always imagined. I've heard it called "smotherhood," but honestly I was so happy that our baby was healthy, and that I was living this dream-come-true of motherhood at last, that I'm quite sure nothing could have taken me away from him for that year and a half.

Change is inevitable, however, and, when Devin was nineteen months old, a consultant finally managed to cajole me into driving with her from Greenville (Texas) to Dallas for a sales meeting. I'm not sure what I was expecting, but when I walked in that room and saw so many of the women with whom I had started in Mary Kay just over two years earlier, I was completely taken aback by the poise, confidence, and success they had achieved. Unlike me, they'd been working their plan, and the improvement was evident. Stranger still, they didn't seem to be woefully unbalanced. Many were talking about their own children and families as though they were normal, healthy, and socially well-adjusted even though these women were doing something other than doting on them twenty-four hours a day. At that moment, the thought that occurred to me for the first time since I had left the hospital with Devin nineteen months earlier was: *maybe this is something I can do along with being a mother and wife.*

Devin, age three.

Of course, I still had no idea what exactly it was I was supposed to be doing. I had managed to maintain active status by making minimum product orders, but then, in 1968, Bruce was transferred from Greenville, Texas, to Greenville, South Carolina (thank God for Mary Kay mobility), and there went the old beauty case into the moving van and on hold again while I got us moved and settled into our new home. In my defense, I had sponsored one woman into the company during the preceding three years, but that had taken up so much of my time I decided never to do it again. Recruiting, the lifeblood of the Mary Kay marketing plan, was totally and completely lost on me at the time.

Shortly after arriving in South Carolina, however, I opened the mail one day to read something that changed my life forever. It was a termination letter from Mary Kay. Friendly enough, the pink

mimeograph paper asked "Can it be true?" and pictured a carica-
ture of data spewing out of a large computer saying "Woe is me!
Doretha Dingler is about to be terminated." The letter continued,
"Even our IBM computer is sad at the thought of the 'possibility'
of your being terminated. We really don't want this to happen."
And it outlined what I needed to do to remain "active" with the
company. The letter was postmarked July 15, 1968, and included
the date when I needed to have my order in: July 31! Friendly or
not, the mere word *termination* got my attention, and I duly noted
the date. It was the first day I ever set a real goal for myself.

Determined to prove how wrong they were to want to terminate me, I started working the phone and somehow convinced
the wives of two people I knew from Bruce's work to host a class
for me. Then, summoning all the courage I could muster and
wearing my best dress, I followed a bit of advice I had received
during one of the few sales meetings I had thus far attended: I

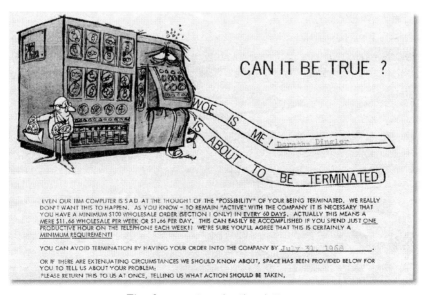

The famous termination letter.

bundled up a huge armful of dry cleaning and went to the neighborhood cleaners where I dropped off the clothes and then asked if I could leave a "facial box," a shoebox with a slit cut in the top that I'd decorated with colorful wrapping paper. My little homemade box proclaimed, "Free. $15 Facial. Register Here." Amazingly enough, that one little box netted me forty appointments from which I recruited twelve people into Mary Kay in one month. I think that was the beginning of my grasping the idea that this was something women wanted, something many of them, like me, really needed.

I guess you could say that sometime in July of 1968 I had my "aha" moment, the moment I realized what was truly possible in Mary Kay, and then things started moving very quickly. During the last three months of 1968 I entered the qualification period for Director, and by January of 1969 (six months after receiving my notice of termination) I was onstage for my Sales Director Debut. Five months after that, our Unit ranked No. 1 in the Mary Kay

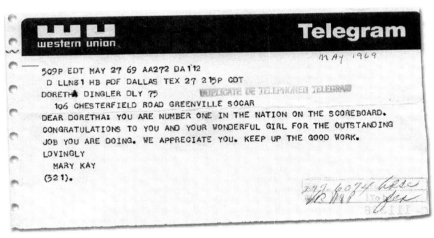

Mary Kay's telegram to me congratulating our Unit for being No. 1 in the nation only five months after our debut.

sales force based on monthly production and became one of the first Units to be recognized as achieving the Half-Million Dollar Unit Club in one year. By the very next year, 1970, I was No. 2 in the nation, and our Unit ranked in the top five every subsequent year until I was named Independent National Sales Director in 1974. All because some computer tried to terminate me.

Bruce and me.

Ever since I retired, the question I'm constantly asked is if I believe I could achieve the same success if I were starting now, if I could replicate this amazing story if I hadn't been, so to speak, on the ground floor joining two years after the company was founded. As I write this, on the eve of the company's fiftieth anniversary, my answer to this question is a resounding yes. Mary Kay is still helping change women's lives around the world because the Mary Kay opportunity, in combination with the Mary Kay value system of God first, family second, career third, works. It worked when Mary Kay founded this company in 1963, and it works in 2012. It worked in Dallas, Texas, and it works in Beijing, China.

> It worked in Dallas, Texas, and it works in Beijing, China.

Though I enjoy a good stroll down memory lane and reminiscing about the "good ole'" days, I believe our best years are ahead of us, and I can't wait to watch the next generation of Mary Kay success stories walk across that stage and blaze an even brighter path for women in the twenty-first century.

My sister
Georgina.

My sister
Glenda.

My brother,
George.

My mother,
Doris.

My paternal grandparents,
Ben and Leota McGee.

My dad, George.

3

How I Became Me

*"Only those who will risk going too far
can possibly find out how far one can go."*
—T. S. ELIOT

For the first ten years of my life, I'd been an only child. I loved school, was a fast learner and an early reader. Then, overnight it seemed to me, our family grew by three and I found myself with two sisters and a brother. After (and maybe because of) that, my dad started taking me to work with him in the summers at his farm-to-market business. He soon found my presence a valuable asset as I became quite astute at estimating the weight of a load of peas brought in by the farmers to sell. I suppose I acquired that skill by observing him bid large acreages of peas in West Texas and then seeing how accurate the bids were when the final product was weighed in and paid

My dad, George, taking a break from his farm-to-market business.

I'm sure that more than one good ol' boy was shocked to have his livelihood determined by a girl not even in high school yet.

for. I was eventually given complete authority to pay the farmers, and I'm sure that more than one good ol' boy was shocked to have his livelihood determined by a girl not even in high school yet.

Maybe it was because of the age difference, or the fact that my parents divorced a year after I married when my sisters and brother were still

Georgina

young, but I always had the feeling that I could somehow help them make that transition in their lives less traumatic. Reflecting on my life as I am now, it seems like maybe those early experiences were more influential than I ever realized. It hadn't occurred to me that these events from my childhood were laying the foundation of the person I would become. I do know that even as a young child I always had the feeling of being responsible (actually there's another story from my childhood I'll talk about later in

Glenda

the book that would come to have a long-range influence on my life as well. I just didn't know how long-range and how profound it would be until much later).

My father had fourteen siblings, so family was everywhere in our small town. My uncle owned a barbershop on the square for fifty years, and I know my dad was

With my parents, my sisters Glenda and Georgina, and my brother, George.

proud of me, but when I was young he would embarrass me to death at the barber shop and around the town square by bragging that I was sooo very smart, a straight-A student, and could beat any of his cronies at checkers (which I could). This may have been the beginning of a genuine belief that I could excel, since my dad not only clearly thought so but seemed to want to tell anyone who would listen as well. I was an honor student, but didn't participate in extracurricular activities because I had to be on the bus for the five-mile trip to our house every afternoon as soon as school let out. In truth, the only activity close enough to home for me to participate in was church, so I went as often as I could and signed up for every event because my cousin Shirley and I could walk there from our house. I loved going to church and, at age twelve, was baptized there but not in a traditional baptistery. As my granddaughter would say, I was baptized "old school" in an actual river near the church. I also loved singing in the choir and playing the piano whenever I could, something I still enjoy today

Me at 16 years old.

as it brings me great comfort. I read once that music is what feelings *sound* like, and that's how playing the piano has always felt to me.

In my day, the girls who didn't marry right out of high school (very few went on to college) were pretty much focused on getting a good job until they could meet Mr. Right. As I mentioned in Chapter 1, even before graduating from high school I had managed to land a great job in the "Big City" (Dallas) and was convinced my destiny was shaping up for the next phase: marriage and family. As it turns out, I had already met my Mr. Right (had in fact been passing him in the hall since sixth grade), but because he was three years older with his own circle of friends, we never dated in high school. By the time I arrived in Dallas, however, Bruce had been honorably discharged from the army due to his father's untimely death (at the age of forty-four) and was working in Dallas, attending night school, working on his engineering degree, and helping his mother and nine-year-old sister.

Bruce's dad, Curtis.

One weekend we both happened to be home visiting and, as fate would have it, attended the same dance at the National Guard Armory in Athens. We had such fun that Bruce asked me out the following week. He says I cancelled the date (honestly I can't remember), but he remained in hot pursuit until we finally started dating. We dated for several months, and then a friend of mine

Bruce with his mom, Lorene, and his sister, Cheri.

(actually one of my roommates) who had decided to move to Midland, Texas, to be closer to her family asked me to join her. I immediately got a job at Shell Oil in Midland with plans to start a new life there, but it was not to be. Bruce Dingler had other plans. He came out to visit me and, to my complete surprise, proposed! Bruce later commemorated our early courtship in a song he wrote for me to celebrate our golden wedding anniversary. "I feel the exact same way about Doretha today as I did when I proposed all those many years ago," he says.

Of course I said "yes," and then one night, a week after we announced our engagement with my photo appearing in the hometown newspaper (luckily saying that a date for the wedding had not been set), we were on an ordinary double date with our good friends Jerry and Sandra when Bruce and I made another huge decision. We decided that rather than have a big wedding, it would be a lot less complicated if we just

The Athens Daily Review

My engagement announcement.

eloped (luckily, Bruce had already received assurances from my dad that he would have no objections to our getting married). Bruce had lost his father a year earlier, and I knew my parents were talking possible divorce. Our friends on the double date weren't even engaged yet, but they decided to take that leap into marriage as well. So, off we drove to neighboring Oklahoma where "spontaneous" marriages were possible.

My granddaughter and I were going through some items in storage a few years ago when I found my "wedding" outfit, a size-

5 navy dress with a white sailor collar. "Dee Dee," she exclaimed, "you were so tiny!" She didn't ask, but I felt compelled to explain to her why we took what might seem like an impulsive step to elope, that it was really for practical reasons. I explained to Brittany that her grandfather was working and going to school at night in one town while I worked in another. Eloping solved several dilemmas we faced, and I related to Brittany something I'd read somewhere that

> "What I was looking for was a *marriage,* not just a wedding ceremony."

seemed to capture my feelings on the subject: "What I was looking for was a *marriage,* not just a wedding ceremony."

Even though it was a hastily arranged event, we did manage to

If I Tried

I have a burning question; I hope you'll answer back.
If I tried to hold you would you—hold me back?
If I tried to kiss you would you—give me a smack?

It started when I shuddered as I watched her dance.
Her moves were so esthetic I was in a trance.
With rhinestone earrings swinging,
And bright brown eyes gleaming,
She let me know I had to take a chance,
Somehow I had to ask this girl to dance.

Every eye was on her; I knew I was a goner.
I had to ask before my cardiac,
If I tried to hold you would you—
hold me back,
If I tried to kiss you would you—
give me a smack?
You have to let me know
Should I stay or go,
Can I celebrate or start to pack?

retain some aspects of a traditional wedding. First and foremost, my co-bride Sandra insisted (and I concurred) that the ceremony be presided over by a minister. So, against all odds, we found a Baptist minister on Easter weekend who was willing to perform our double Easter Sunday Oklahoma wedding. Also, one of Jerry and Bruce's college friends happened to be home visiting that weekend, so we had a best man to boot.

We couples remain lifelong friends, and to this day we laugh because when the minister asked, "Do you take this woman to be your lawful wedded wife?" Jerry said, "We do." Well, there must have been some magic in the air that Easter Sunday because, like us, the Hollands are still married. I'm also happy to report that the same newspaper that announced our engagement was still around

12A Athens Daily Review

Bruce and Doretha Dingler

Our golden anniversary announcement.

to carry our golden anniversary announcement—only this time Bruce is pictured with me!

Jerry and Sandra Holland— our wedding partners.

Out to dinner with Merwyn and Polly Pickle. Bruce and Merwyn have been best friends since high school.

Life was good in that first year of marriage. Bruce was working, and for one semester we both attended night classes at Arlington State College (now University of Texas at Arlington). Our first little rental house was on a street in Arlington called, appropriately enough, Lovers Lane. We quickly decided, however, that Bruce should take advantage of the GI Bill and transfer to Texas Tech University in Lubbock, where he could

Harold and Peggy Larison—great friends from E-Systems

complete the engineering degree he'd begun there before going into the army. In order to help put Bruce through college, I went to work in the office of the Dean of Arts and Sciences where they trained me to be a degree counselor. The year he graduated from Tech, the university offered *him* a teaching fellowship position so *I'd* remain in my job! It wasn't to be, though, and we left Lubbock armed with newly accorded degrees: his, a degree in math and engineering, and mine a PHTS—"Putting Hubby Through School." Yes, that was an actual document they offered supportive

wives in those days. It was very "official" looking, signed by the college president with the Texas Tech gold seal affixed, and today this charming little sign of the times hangs next to Bruce's diploma from Tech and his Sigma Alpha Epsilon (SAE) fraternity plaque in our office. My citation declares that I was recognized for "having completed in a most satisfactory and effective manner the major project of:

"aiding, babying, consoling, driving, egging, feeding, goading, helping, imploring, joking, kicking, loving, martyring, nagging, offending, pitying, quieting, renouncing, satisfying, tutoring, urging, vilifying, worshipping, yelling, and otherwise abetting her husband in the pursuit of a baccalaureate degree from this College."

I repeat all those words here because they show better than anything just how far society has come, how much has changed, and how very different the landscape is today for women. When Mary Kay Ash formed the company of her dreams in 1963, she often said her vision in founding the company was to give women the opportunities they'd been denied. Honestly, I don't think that many of us were actually aware at the time we had been "denied" anything; we just plain didn't even consider that building a business would ever be in our realm of possibility. But that's why

> I believe our world in the early sixties needed precisely what she was about to offer women. We just didn't know it yet!

Mary Kay Ash is so often described as a visionary leader and why the term "possibility thinker" fits her to a tee. Looking back, I believe our world in the early sixties needed precisely what she was about to offer women. We just didn't know it yet!

My brother George, age 12.

When Bruce landed his first engineering job after college in Greenville, Texas, we settled happily into our new hometown. With no children of our own, we welcomed my brother George at age eleven to make his home with us, and he remained with us until graduating from high school and entering college. We were delighted for the opportunity to help my mother and be part of my brother's development. He was a great athlete, loved sports, played football, and loved his animals (a horse named Lady and his dog, Prince).

My mother, who had moved from Athens to be near her sister in Austin and to accept a job with the state (from which she retired twenty years later), was a single working mom struggling with parenting two teenage daughters and a preteen son. Turns out she had actually been quite a saleswoman in her younger years. She sold ornate silverware for a direct sales com-

Doris Crecelius—my mother's senior high school yearbook photo.

pany, but with one car and little spousal support, she never actively pursued that career, despite winning several sales awards and certificates of achievement. I found these awards with her belongings after her death. I have few pictures of my mother from her early years, but a few years ago, to my complete surprise and amazement, a book came out about our hometown of Athens, Texas, and there, for whatever reason, was a picture of the Athens High School senior class of 1936 featuring a beautiful eighteen-year-old Doris Crecelius, my mother.

Georgina and Glenda

I always loved being big sister to my siblings. My sisters, Glenda and Georgina, were only fourteen months apart in age and as different as night and day. That's what made them so much fun. I used to dress them in lookalike dresses at Easter, with George in his Easter suit, and off we'd go after church on our Easter egg hunt.

It is one of the happiest memories I have of our early years together. Later, Glenda would go on to earn her cosmetology license and eventually become a real estate agent while Georgina went to college for her nursing degree (R.N.) and was very close to finishing when she decided to pursue her passion for ministry work. My brother now owns his own ranch and is a success-ful entrepreneur-owner of UPS franchises.

With my brother George and Mary Kay.

Two years later, while still in Greenville, Texas, Bruce and two other engineers, Jackie Martin and Bob Weems, decided to become part-time real estate developers. They purchased twenty-three acres near E-Systems (an aerospace/ engineering firm where they all worked) and created a first-of-its-kind residential development with all-underground utilities and deed restrictions as to home size, outbuildings, etc. They named it Wildwood Estates, and that's where we built our first real home. One of our friends who still lives there, Dot Warren, says that even after all these years the house is still referred to as "the Dingler Place." Jackie and Bob's wives, Evelyn and

With Devin showing off my brother George's first car in 1969.

Going native with the Martins
and the Weems.

Pam, along with Dot, would later be instrumental in hosting my first Mary Kay parties.

Little did we know as we were going about our everyday lives back then that our future course was about to be irrevocably altered by something as seemingly innocuous as a wig party. They say the Lord works in mysterious ways, and I am certainly living proof of that. If I hadn't been so late for that first wig party, I might not have been as determined to have the full experience at the next one, which led to my signing a Consultant agreement. If I'd gotten pregnant when I'd wanted, I certainly wouldn't have committed to anything that might interfere with impending motherhood, like joining a new company. And if Mary Kay hadn't reassured us all that we could put God first, family second, career third, and still be successful in this business, I never would have stuck with it after Devin was born. In hindsight, it seems like God, and Mary Kay, knew what they were doing all along. They just had to wait for me to catch up.

Dot Warren, who hosted my first Mary Kay party in Greenville, Texas.

Loving the product only further reinforced the fact that with Mary Kay I had finally found that "something" I had been searching for, a place where I could grow personally and professionally but where family priorities could take precedence over the j.o.b.

Interestingly enough, there have been several research studies that explain those positive feelings I experienced as part of Mary Kay's pioneer generation. One study reports that what today's young women seem to crave most in their work is the very thing I found more than four decades ago: work that "enhances their personal life." I read another study recently that talked about the importance of associating with positive people and the long-term beneficial effect that has on one's psyche. In terms of happiness and positive outlook over the course of a lifetime, the intrinsic value of the Mary Kay experience has undoubtedly added years to my life and life to my years, as they say. These influences altered my entire life trajectory and that of my family, and I truly cannot imagine better influences than I found within the Mary Kay sisterhood of friends.

> . . . in that era a married woman couldn't get such a loan—it had to be co-signed by her husband.

I was also fortunate in that Bruce was 100 percent supportive of my endeavors, as I had always been with his. The only monetary investment I ever made in my business was a $400 loan from our bank in Greenville, Texas. Actually, it was a business loan made *to* Bruce *for me.* You see, in that era a married woman couldn't get such a loan—it had to be *co-signed by her husband.* That loan agreement holds a special place next to the first of several plaques I received when I broke the *$10 million mark* in overall commissions. Wall Street would call that a good return on investment.

> The only monetary investment I ever made in my business was a $400 loan from our bank in Greenville, Texas.

In addition to being a good investment, that loan is yet another great example of the kind of valuable lessons Mary Kay taught us about how to establish ourselves as business owners. She knew that in order to truly grow our business we would need to have commercial credit with a local bank. To accomplish this, she suggested that we get to know a banker in our town, apply for a loan (whether we needed the money or not), and then pay it back early as a way of proving we were serious.

My first (and last) bank loan.

A good return on investment.

After we relocated to Greenville, South Carolina, in 1968, I fully expected to continue my Mary Kay business in as low key a manner as I had in Greenville, Texas. Once I received that now-famous termination letter shortly after our arrival, however, I knew it was time for me to step up and show up. Fortunately, once I made that decision, God put some wonderful women in my life without whom this story would not have been possible. I was particularly blessed to have a woman in my unit who would become my fellow trailblazer in a part of the country that at the time had a poor economy and dim prospects for improvement.

> God put some wonderful women in my life without whom this story would not have been possible.

South Carolina was so traditionally southern that in the late sixties it wasn't considered a good environment for women in business. Mary Kay told me years later that she knew the weak prognostications about southern states, but when she saw what I (her first Sales Director in South Carolina) was doing, she wasn't about to dampen our enthusiasm because of research to the contrary. Once she saw what was happening, she knew we were on to something and began to encourage me to share the story of our success.

Bruce was, again, to be my lucky charm. Not only did he willingly help with Devin and whatever was needed after 4:30 every afternoon, but it was his E-Systems contacts in South Carolina, just as it was in Texas, that helped me rekindle my Mary Kay business. Soon after my "inspiration" (termination) letter arrived, the daughter-in-law of a top executive of E-Systems agreed to book a Mary Kay show for me and invited her friends, which was another huge turning point, because in that class was an educated and poised young lady who would go on to become my lifelong friend and very first offspring Sales Director (the aforementioned trailblazer). She helped me build the unit that was about to make Mary Kay Ash and everyone at the corporate headquarters in Dallas sit up and take notice. Her banker father and grandfather had taught her to understand money matters, and so this genteel southern lady was a virtual gold mine when it came to teaching me to run my business on a sound financial basis. Nan Stroud was (and is) a great teacher, motivator, and true daughter of South Carolina to whom I'll always be indebted.

With Mary Kay at my first
Seminar Awards Night.

The South Carolina Unit
Dressed and ready for our first Seminar
Awards Night.

4

"Keys to Success"—
A Life-Changing Speech

"Courage is knowing what not to fear."
—PLATO

*I*n Chapter 1, I told you about that first speech, the "deal-killer," as my son would say. I also told you about my brilliant plan to avoid any chance of a repeat performance by staying out of the "Top Ten" and therefore off the stage at the largest annual gathering of the Mary Kay sales force, called Seminar. Well, wouldn't you know it, soon after my return to South Carolina, still recovering from that harrowing experience in Dallas, I found out I had in fact broken into the Top Ten and therefore had to make another speech, only this time it wouldn't be to a few dozen Directors

With Mary Kay at a Seminar Awards Night.

but to the hundreds of attendees at Seminar (those of you attending one of the five separate Seminars held today that sell out the entire Dallas Convention Center may find it hard to believe we used to be able to conduct the entire event over the course of a few days in a hotel ballroom).

Looking back now it's almost comical, but living it was not funny at all. I'd always told myself I wanted no part of any job that required either of two things: public speaking or flying in airplanes. Well, I had so far managed to avoid flying thanks to Bruce generously

> I'd always told myself I wanted no part of any job that required either of two things: public speaking or flying in airplanes.

taking time off from work to drive me. And, as nervous as I was, I somehow managed to survive that first hour-long speech, and it was enough of a success to put the idea of quitting on hold, at least for a little while. But when I received the "Big One"—an official invitation to be a keynote speaker onstage at Seminar—I was terrified. The telegram arrived one afternoon, and by the time Bruce came home from work that evening I was beside myself. I thrust that yellow Western Union at him like all of this was *his* fault, and informed him, once again, of my intention to quit because I could see that being associated with this company was nothing but flying and making speeches and I wanted no part of it!

Once again Bruce pitched his now-getting-a-little-old proposal of "just go to Dallas and make this one speech, then quit" knowing that I would take the bait. Bruce knew that I was eventually going to have to face these fears head-on, but in the interim he cleverly convinced me to take just one more step, face just one more fear before breaking and running for cover. Next he moved to phase two of his evil plan and enrolled me in a Dale Carnegie speaking course. Now, I still don't know if it was because he wanted to be sure I actually attended, being the only woman enrolled in the class, or for his own benefit, but Bruce Dingler—varsity football player, class president, voted most popular in high school his senior year, and self-assured engineer with a promising career—also signed himself up for the course. I didn't believe for a minute that he needed three months of Dale Carnegie, but *I* certainly did and can admit now that I was grateful to have him there, right there between me and the door so I couldn't bolt when it was my turn to speak. To make a long and terrifying story short, we both survived/finished the course and still have our Dale Carnegie diplomas to prove it. I encourage anyone to take the course if, like me, you have a fear of public speaking or simply want to improve your skills. It is well worth the time and money invested and will give you a boost in confidence that will benefit every area of your personal and professional life.

When I finally made it onto the stage in Dallas to deliver that first major Seminar speech, I was given a tip by one of the Mary Kay staff to have the lights on the audience very low and to flood

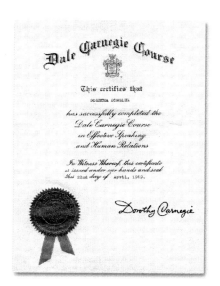

the stage so that I really couldn't see the audience—and it worked! I couldn't see a thing except the notes in my trembling hand. And so, with the audience blacked out and the ink still wet on my Dale Carnegie diploma, I was able to muster the courage to deliver my first major speech: "Keys to Success." To this day I hold one indelible memory in my mind. It's the memory of walking off that stage, where the first person at the bottom of the stairs to greet and congratulate me was Mary Kay Ash. If I had any remaining doubts about speaking or sharing my experience from the stage, they were quelled the instant I saw the pride in Mary Kay's eyes as she enveloped me in one of her famous hugs. In fact, Mary Kay liked the speech so much that she asked if she could print it in the "Consultant's Guide," then a simple mimeographed booklet full of tips to help the sales force succeed (it's also included at the end of this chapter). I left Seminar that day having been transformed by the strength of Mary Kay's belief in me. I remember thinking *Wow! If Mary Kay herself believes I have something to offer, then maybe, just maybe, I really do.* And the rest, as they say, is history.

No one was more surprised than me by how well "Keys to Success" was received at the 1969 Seminar. Maybe it was beginner's luck, or maybe it was just that I had a fresh perspective by virtue of being a new Director in the company that allowed me to crystallize my thoughts on what it would take to succeed in this business, but to be honest, at the time it felt a little like building an airplane while I was flying it. These were not the sage reflections of some battle-hardened veteran; these were reports straight from the front lines as I and my unit tried, failed, and tried again to lead, encourage, and grow what would ultimately become the Dingler Area.

> Bruce arranged for me to board a commercial airliner and meet with the pilot and co-pilot in the cockpit.

As for my fear of public speaking, from that day in 1969 until my retirement in 2003, I never again attended Seminar without taking the podium at least once. Fortunately, I was able to grow in experience and confidence as the sales force grew in number so that by the time I was speaking to thousands instead of hundreds of Seminar attendees, I had grown accustomed to the larger audience (though I still liked to keep them "in the dark" so to speak).

I still had to address one more fear before I could truly soar in my career, however: my fear of flying. Coming to the rescue once again, Bruce arranged for me to board a commercial airliner and meet with the pilot and co-pilot in the cockpit while the passengers were boarding. To say the least, it was a very informative session. I was given a very detailed explanation, in layperson's terms, about what happens during takeoff, landing, and everything in between. Since Bruce was already well acquainted with most aspects of aviation, having flown electronic testing equipment on C-130 aircraft for E-Systems, he was able to continue the

Fearlessly flying the Concord from Paris to New York with Mary Kay (and, coincidentally, Mary Tyler Moore).

conversation and reinforce the message that flying was perfectly safe. The combination of having solid, detailed information reinforced by someone I loved and trusted helped to ease some of my fears. One great husband—two huge fears addressed!

Of course, anyone who does a lot of flying knows there are going to be moments that test the mettle of even the most seasoned air traveler. I can remember one trip from South Carolina to Los Angeles, with the obligatory stopover in Atlanta, of course, during which the pilot announced the following over the intercom: "Folks, we're out of gas and I am going to have to find somewhere to land this plane." As it turned out, we were on a 727, which normally holds enough fuel to fly from Atlanta to Los Angeles with ease, but because we had encountered heavy head winds we were running low, and to make matters worse, due to heavy fog in Los Angeles the airport had been closed. Although the pilot had attempted to divert to other airports close by, they too were closing before he could get cleared for landing. At this point the closest airport still open was Las Vegas, but we didn't have enough gas to get there either. Though I admired his candor, I questioned the pilot's judgment as he shared with us every detail of our ever-worsening dilemma—not that we needed much explanation as the fog

it is awe-inspiring and wonderful to watch, but you'd better get out of the way once it happens!

was so thick we could hardly see the wings of the plane. Finally, he simply informed us, "We have to land this aircraft, so be prepared." As you can imagine, my fellow passengers and I were terrified as we "prepared" for the worst. Luckily, we had reduced our altitude enough that the pilot was able to visually locate a safe place to land, on a remote runway that was actually connected to the L.A. airport system. Once on the ground, it seemed like we taxied forever to finally get to our destination, but nobody minded now that we were safely back on terra firma.

Of course, the real lesson I learned by facing my (then) two biggest fears was that any fear could be overcome with a little strategy and a lot of support. Because of Mary Kay's belief in me and her ability to get me to face my fears, I came to realize that if I ever intended to become a leader, encouraging women to move beyond whatever was holding them back, then I had to first overcome the things holding *me* back. Only then could I truly understand and be able to give other women what they need to become successful. Mary Kay showed me how this simple act of conveying to another person that you really, truly, unflinchingly believe in them and their ability to succeed can release potential along the same magnitude as splitting an atom to release energy: it is awe-inspiring and wonderful to watch, but you'd better get out of the way once it happens!

> You must find your confidence, get out of your comfort zone, and overcome your fears— whatever it is that's holding you back from doing what you want to do in your life.

If I have any message to impart that might help you be successful, I'd have to first advise that you must find your confidence, get out of your comfort zone, and overcome your fears—whatever it is that's holding you back from doing what you want to do in your life. I remember one year in my keynote speech talking on the subject of how comfort zones can be dangerous, confining places. I was speaking, of course, from personal experience.

What Does She Have That I Can't Have Fixed?

The second important lesson is to work on your self-esteem. Mary Kay always told us that lack of confidence is the greatest barrier women face, and she was fully aware of how that could be affected by a woman's self-esteem. In my case, I had been a five-cigarette-a-day smoker (a great pastime while playing bridge). In the mid-1960s when the surgeon general's warning about the hazards of cigarettes came out, however, I quit cold turkey. I had also become increasingly self-conscious about the small space between my two front teeth, so with some of the first money I earned from Mary Kay, I got my teeth fixed (it also helped that one of the women in my Unit was married to an excellent dentist whom I already knew and trusted). I can't tell you what a difference these two simple "fixes" made in my self-esteem.

I think that's one of the reasons why Mary Kay liked to encourage us to talk about overcoming our fears and sharing our self-esteem issues. She even came up with a name for it: an *I Story*. She asked us to always remember that people relate best to, and learn the most from, personal stories. Accordingly, the story of our life was considered as important for us to recount as any product information. Mary Kay knew that each time we repeated our life story, there would be women hearing it who truly could relate. She always wanted us to remember where we came from, knowing that each of us had a unique story that could inspire someone. For more than four decades, my termination-letter story has given hope to so many women

Picture of me in Mary Kay's earliest recruiting brochures with my "I Story" titled "There's No Business Like Show Business," 1970.

who've had something happen to derail their career. It's given hope to all those women in the audience who felt like one failure spelled doom, and that led them to conclude they should just throw in the towel. I also learned to speak openly about my "smotherhood" tendencies, the bad habits I had to break, and the importance of owning and fixing anything that was weighing down my self-esteem.

Through my association with thousands of women in various settings and countries over the years, I've received validation of how they gravitate to these types of stories. They are good examples to have when others—even well-meaning relatives and, yes, even husbands—try to define the parameters of what they can achieve. I'm adamant in my refusal to believe that you're ever too old, too young, too late, too educated, too pretty, or too shy to get better. The sooner you get your head on straight about that, the sooner you can be successful. Mary Kay said it so often: "This business is between your ears." She knew, and frequently reminded us, that it's impossible to predict a woman's success based on background, looks, age, personality, education, or any other trait besides sheer will. I often spoke on this topic myself and, as my favorite example, I used the amazing fact of Abraham Lincoln's thirty years of virtual failure before he finally succeeded in becoming president of the United States.

> Always remember that people relate best to, and learn the most from, personal stories.

Molding a Life Is a Joyous Thing

I was fortunate to have as a friend and mentor the late Helen McVoy, who joined Mary Kay the same year I did and whose success as one of the first two Independent National Sales Directors (NSDs or Nationals) always inspired me. She believed that goal setting was an absolute prerequisite for success. She thought, for instance, that everyone attending a Mary Kay event should leave with a goal. "If you leave without a goal, it'll take you *two weeks* to recover from this meeting," she'd tell us. "But if you establish a goal before you leave, you'll be amazed at how *two hours* will be ample time for you to recover and get on with your business." Helen was so right: we all need a goal to work toward.

Helen also taught me to have fun and enjoy this career, as she did (I'll tell you a story later that perfectly illustrates that spirit). I was so humbled when Helen's daughter called me after her mother died in 2008 to ask that I deliver her eulogy. I must admit that the idea of getting up before that audience to speak about a best friend of Mary Kay, and one of the first women to become a National Sales Director, brought back some of my early public speaking fears. I concluded this was Mary Kay and Helen's way of reminding me that even when you think you've done it all, there are still opportunities to grow. I consented, of course, and as I ascended the podium that day I looked for a sign from those two beloved women who had been such great teachers, friends, and role models. I'll always miss their hugs and words of encouragement and hope I never forget to provide that same level of encouragement to others.

> You can work hard and work smart as long as you have three things: a proven method, a great product, and a real opportunity to progress.

Taking Helen's goal setting a step further, one year I paid to bring ten of my top Sales Directors to Dallas for a meeting. I needed to see who among them really had the desire to move forward with their businesses. It was an up-close way for me to check their commitment and to find out what I could do to help them achieve their goals. It's funny telling this now, but one of those women told me years later that her husband was utterly shocked that his wife would be invited to attend such a retreat. In fact, he'd convinced her that he had figured out why I invited her. He thought I either wanted to fire her (which I couldn't do since she was an independent contractor) or convince her to cut her hair! He wouldn't have minded if Joanne had come home from that trip having given up her Mary Kay business, but he absolutely did not want her to cut her hair.

Whatever business you're in, I believe that you can work hard and work smart as long as you have three things: a proven method, a great product, and a real opportunity to progress. One of my favorite things about the Mary Kay business is that there's always a new goal to strive for. You never feel like you have it all but, rather, that you need to continue to learn and grow each year. Like athletes, the veterans and the rookies start over every season. The slate is wiped clean and everyone has the opportunity to prove themselves once again. When people ask me the secret to my success, I say I learned how to work, how to build, how to grow, and how to thrive, and every year I'd start over, doing those exact same things but with a new goal. Throughout my career, from the very first Seminar I attended, I would set my goals by what I learned from that annual meeting, and I encouraged my Unit, and later my Area, to do the same.

I constantly preached my belief in taking small steps that help you achieve your goals. We got accustomed to setting incremental goals, eating the elephant one bite at a time, as Zig Ziglar would say. I discouraged new Sales Directors from talking about earning a car until they had reached the necessary growth milestones along the way. When the goals become more realistic, they're more attainable. Without fail, as each new goal was achieved, the belief barriers would begin to break down.

> We got accustomed to setting incremental goals, eating the elephant one bite at a time, as Zig Ziglar would say.

One of our most successful area promotions was something we called the "400 Club." It was a way to encourage enough sales to ensure what we referred to as car production (i.e., 400 wholesale orders of $250 earned a pink Cadillac that year), but we never mentioned that. I wanted more than anything to be sure my Unit was working for something beyond *my* goals. I became quite adept at discovering what a woman was best at, then encouraging her to do it. We still laugh today when we recall some of the contests we came up with to keep the work fun but challenging. One time I made the mistake of seeking Bruce's help to create a contest for my Area. It took a slide rule to figure out that contest! Needless to say, that was one contest no one could get excited about since no one could figure it out. Remember that the first Texas Instruments calculator had just been invented in 1967, and those early models cost several thousand dollars. We didn't have them at our fingertips as we do now. Even so, I still recommend keeping it simple.

As we helped women set achievable goals, more of them began to believe they could succeed. The fabric of American life was undergoing major changes in those days, when it was an accomplishment just to persuade the women in my Unit there were many good business reasons why they needed to be sure to attend our weekly sales meetings. Most housewives were of the opinion that their expertise extended only as far as the kitchen, living room, and bedroom. The ones who did have jobs outside the home were accustomed to being told when to go to lunch, when to use the restroom and for how long, and never to use the telephone for personal business. More often than not, a woman who wanted to attend a Mary Kay sales meeting in the early days would have to convince her husband that a home-cooked dinner might not be on the table at 6:00 that night, and he'd need to have charge of the children as soon as he got home from work. Against that backdrop, can you imagine how the thought of a woman leaving her family to attend a company meeting a thousand miles away in Dallas went over? Leaving the nest for an evening was a long-enough shot, but traveling solo, spending grocery money for hotel and airfare, was quite another. To make it a little more palatable (and in some cases just to make it possible), we established a little fund whereby each woman could deposit a small sum weekly so that by Seminar she'd have enough to fly to Dallas and stay in a hotel. (I devote an entire chapter later in this book to how we got the husbands on board in the early days because I believe these skills are as important today as they were then.)

In 1970, when we were the No. 2 sales unit in the nation, more than half the women who traveled to Dallas with my group had never flown before, and many had never traveled without a parent or a husband accompanying them. As leaders, we also were learning, as evidenced by the fact that the first time we brought a large group to Dallas, we hadn't budgeted enough in the travel savings account for eating evening meals out (Mary Kay provided breakfast and lunch with conference registration). We decided the best thing to do was to gather in my hotel room while Bruce found some kind of takeout food for everyone. He brought thirty hamburgers into our room at the Fairmont Hotel but forgot to have the burger joint leave off the onions, so the scent of onions permeated our hotel room for the duration of Seminar. The memory of those onions and that pungent smell kept me humble years later when our catered banquets filled Dallas hotel ballrooms.

> I devote an entire chapter later in this book to how we got the husbands on board . . .

Part Psychologist, Part Businesswoman

Another key factor in our success was what Mary Kay taught us about the importance of reading people well. I can recall like it was yesterday how Mary Kay drummed into us that we should "never have dollar signs in our eyes."

She'd say we needed to become an expert at figuring out what it was a woman wanted from us, not vice versa. She'd teach us when we'd go to their homes, for instance, to observe how they lived, determine what were the important things to them and their families, even note what they had hanging on their walls. "Find out what she's passionate about, and you'll find out what motivates her," she'd say. I remember one Beauty Consultant who was determined to quit. This devoted mother couldn't stand the fact that her nine-year-old daughter cried every time she had to go out to an appointment or skin care class. After visiting with the woman, I found out that her daughter loved horses and wanted desperately to have a horse of her own. So we devised a little savings account. The mother explained to her daughter that each time she needed to be out of the house for business, if the daughter could avoid a crying tantrum, the mother would deposit $5 into this fund and that the money would be used to purchase a horse. The tactic worked. The girl was happy, the mom was productive, and it wasn't long before their little family increased by one—one horse, that is.

Part of reading people well also comes from knowing when their attitude is going to be a deterrent. I had another Beauty Consultant who was so extremely negative that she was dragging others down with her. She just couldn't seem to find success and blamed everyone but herself. Worse than that, she wanted everyone else to feel bad with her. I've found that women are especially susceptible to this kind of group dynamic, and it can be toxic. This particular woman had been a nurse before starting her Mary Kay business, and one evening at our sales meeting, when she'd depressed everyone with her especially negative comments, I had finally had enough. "If this business is so bad," I said, "maybe you should return to nursing." Something must have clicked after that because she stopped being so negative, and it wasn't long before she finally learned how great a business Mary Kay could be. From then on, our code word around the house when I felt someone wasn't right for this business was "maybe she should return to nursing."

And speaking of other careers, we knew we were trailblazing by pursuing Mary Kay as our full-time profession, and it was often a slippery slope convincing others to join us. When a woman already has another job but is interested in a Mary Kay business, it can become quite an issue as to when she decides to give up that steady paycheck—no matter how meager—and rely entirely on the income from her Mary Kay business. Mary Kay knew that an unsuccessful Beauty Consultant is an unhappy one, so she made sure we didn't encourage women to leave their jobs until they were certain they could replace the income with Mary Kay earnings. Part of experiencing success took learning the discipline of working from home.

> . . . we knew we were trailblazing by pursuing Mary Kay as our full-time profession

Mary Kay said being willing to "wake up to a dark neighborhood where everyone else's lights are still off" and begin your workday earlier than everyone else, when it would be so easy to sleep in, required a certain discipline, especially for women used to punching a clock in a traditional work setting. To facilitate this transition, Mary Kay came up with the Five O'clock Club and encouraged those who needed a few extra hours every day to "join" her early morning club! Of course, there was also the discipline required to get out of our nightgowns and actually dress for work even when we were only commuting from the bedroom to the kitchen table in the morning.

And then there was the telephone. Mary Kay wanted us to be

careful how we spent our telephone time, aware as she was of how it could undermine a productive day (I imagine she'd have the same sentiment about texting, e-mailing, and social networking). "Have some urgency in your voice when you make a call," she'd tell us, "and let the caller know you haven't got time for idle chatter." She advised us to get a sand timer to keep our calls under three minutes. And yes, she even endorsed getting household or secretarial help when our business could support it.

Mary Kay saw how women new to working from home had trouble organizing and prioritizing their lives when moving from a traditional work environment. Because she knew this was essential to their success, for three years in a row she asked that I teach a class on how to get organized (though I always wondered if that wasn't as much to help me as the attendees).

Another critical aspect of working from home that Mary Kay understood all too well was that our families were watching. Her own three children had helped her count the change from her sales in the earliest days of her first direct selling experience with Stanley Home Products, and her son Richard often told the story about how if they'd made more one week than the last, his mom would treat the kids to a movie. Mary Kay knew how important it was to get our families on board with what we were doing and how important it was we share the goals we had for our business. Without that support, she knew our families could be our biggest obstacles, but with it they could be our greatest cheerleaders.

> Mary Kay knew how important it was to get our families on board with what we were doing . . .

That lesson is one of the most important I ever learned from Mary Kay, and it would become a centerpiece of my success. It's so important, in fact, that I devote an entire chapter in this book to the topic. What I discovered was that there were lots of women out there for whom the "comfort zone" of home and hearth was more like a jail than a refuge. They, like me, longed for something of their own. They were willing to work hard to make a better life for their families given the opportunity. This was something the rest of the business world had ignored to its detriment by relegating women to "their place" at the bottom of the corporate ladder, if indeed they were on it at all. I recall Mary Kay's grandson Ryan Rogers defining this so well when early in the new century he accepted Mary Kay's posthumous award as the Greatest Female Entrepreneur in American History. "Grandmother," Ryan said, "captured the hearts and the minds of women."

It's so true. Mary Kay didn't just talk about the need for change. She did something about it and was perhaps one of the first to have a real, positive impact helping women. Many decades later, she would provide her definition of a great day as something like this: "If today one more woman discovers her God-given talent, how great she really is, then it's been a great day for me."

> When Mary Kay founded her company, minimum wage hovered around $1

Business scholars have long since credited Mary Kay with the economic liberation of women at a time when glass ceilings weren't even acknowledged, much less talked about as a social issue. When Mary Kay founded her company, minimum wage hovered around $1 and the average salary for most of the decade of the 1960s was under $5,000 a year. Well, by the late 1960s I had already deposited one $2,500 monthly check, but, much more than raising our family income, that kind of earning potential had raised my consciousness. By the time I heard the words to the 1971 hit anthem "I Am Woman," I had already found my voice.

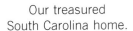

Our treasured
South Carolina home.

My favorite
thing: hosting
one of Devin's
birthday parties
on our deck in
South Carolina.

My therapy—my music.

Having fun on my
motorcycle.

KEYS TO SUCCESS—First Seminar Speech, 1969

I. KEY NO. 1—STUDY YOUR MANUAL

    A. The manual is an inspired guideline to all the facets of our job.

    B. It is based on 25 years of experience.

    C. Without the basic knowledge of our profession, we cannot even attempt to attain success.

    D. I recommend that each new Consultant read the manual 10 times the first week, before and after each of her first five shows.

    E. The second week, she should read it before each Show, and at least twice a week thereafter.

    F. The answers are all there if we will take the time to search for them.

    G. Have you ever thought what we would do if we didn't have this great Manual?

Reading your manual is one of the first KEYS TO SUCCESS.

II. KEY NO. 2—BOOKING YOUR SHOWS

    A. Booking has often been described as being the "lifeline" of our business . . . and this is true . . . because, if you can't Book, you're out of business.

    B. In order to keep a full date book, you should know the following:

    The correct booking approach . . . which is in your manual.

    The tentative date booking talk . . . which is in your manual.

    The answers to the most frequently heard "booking excuses" . . . which are in your manual. (Remember, when a woman says NO . . . she means maybe . . . when she says MAYBE . . . she means yes . . . oftentimes she is simply saying, "TELL ME MORE."

    C. You should also learn to:

        1. Book in close . . . never more than 3 weeks ahead.

        2. Always book the first part of the week first, and from these you can book the last of the week.

3. Use X'd out booking plan . . . which is described in your manual.

4. Always book more for each week than you really want to hold . . . for insurance . . . Book 7 to hold 5.

D. Finally, carry the little "before and after" cards with you for Conversational Booking. IN BOOKING, WORRY ABOUT ONLY ONE THING . . . HOW MANY SHOWS DO I HAVE BOOKED FOR NEXT WEEK??

And remember to look for bookings everywhere . . .

1. At your shows
2. Grocery stores
3. Department stores
4. Anywhere there are people

Be ever aware that bookings are all around you,
because this is another important KEY to your SUCCESS.

III. KEY NO. 3—SERVICE YOUR CUSTOMERS

A. We are building our very own Mary Kay business, and the most important thing about a sale is that we keep the customer from now on, and we do this by servicing our Customers.

B. That first sale has often been described as just the preliminary return on our investment and with every re-order, our profit and our business grows.

C. Give your customers the same service that you would expect.

D. Periodically, ask yourself these questions:

1. Have I done everything possible to service my customers to the best of my ability, at all times?

2. Have I called my pink tickets?

3. Have I kept all my promises?

4. Have I taken care of my customers' problems without hesitation?

5. Have I always delivered on time?

If you can truthfully answer these questions "Yes" . . . you are SERVICING
YOUR CUSTOMERS which is another KEY to your SUCCESS.

IV. KEY NO. 4—PLAN YOUR TIME

Robert Ripley, the "Believe It or Not" man, once pointed out:

"A plain bar of iron is worth $5."

"This same bar of iron, when made into horseshoes, is worth $10.50."

"If made into needles, it is worth $355."

"If made into pen knife blades, it is worth $3,285."

"If turned into balance springs for watches, that identical bar of iron becomes worth $250,000."

The same is true of TIME.

You won't find it in your wallet or your bank account.

You can't borrow it.

You can't work harder and earn more of it; and certainly you can't hoard it.

In fact, all you can do with it is spend it.

TIME is the universal coin of achievement, equally available to all.

Some people can turn an hour into horseshoes.

Others can turn it into needles.

A smaller number know how to change it into knife blades.

But only a few have learned how to transform a golden hour into true-tempered watch springs.

**What you do with your time will largely depend on
how successful you become in Mary Kay.**

V. KEY NO. 5—RECRUITING

A. It has often been said that RECRUITING is the only way you can be truly SUCCESSFUL, because you multiply yourself through others.

Wise is the man who realizes early in life that what he can do in and of himself is small indeed . . . but what he can do by working with and properly influencing others is almost miraculous.

B. So—Learn the 4 Point Recruiting Plan:

1. Before every Show, ASK "Who is coming today who might be interested in doing what I do?"

2. Put on a crackerjack Recruiting Talk at the beginning of each Show . . . TELL YOUR STORY.

3. Select ONE person at every Show, and offer her your job.

4. Promise the Hostess $5 in merchandise for any person who is accepted by the Company and goes to work that she suggests.

IT IS EASIER NOW TO RECRUIT THAN EVER BEFORE . . .

PEOPLE EVERYWHERE ARE THRILLED WITH OUR PRODUCT AND EAGER TO SHARE THE MARY KAY OPPORTUNITY.

RECRUIT everywhere you go BECAUSE this is another very important KEY to your SUCCESS.

VI. KEY NO. 6—ENTHUSIASM

A. Put a barrel of enthusiasm and determination into everything you do.

B. Approach each new day with the excitement and the will to make the very most of that day.

C. With enthusiasm, you will not only become a better Consultant, but a happier person.

As you reach perfection in each of these areas, you will find that SUCCESS is in the palm of your hand. REMEMBER:

Study your manual . . . Book your shows

Service your customers . . . Stay on your toes

Plan your time . . . Recruit your kin

Add a lot of enthusiasm . . . And a will to win

With all these ingredients . . . That I suggest

You, my friends . . . Have the KEYS TO SUCCESS!

Mary Kay and her three children, Ben, Marilyn, and Richard in the early years of the company.

With Mary Kay's grandson, Ryan Rogers

Erma Thomson, Mary Kay's longtime assistant

Mel Ash, Mary Kay's husband

With Ryan's mother, Jan

5

The Sue Vickers Story—
The Original "Miss Go-Give"

"Every silver lining has a cloud."
—MARY KAY ASH

Though I pride myself in being able to stay upbeat in almost any situation, there were times in my career when even I found it very difficult to remain positive. One of those times was when I learned about the death of my friend and fellow National Sales Director Sue Vickers (in fact, Sue and I debuted as Nationals together in 1974).

With Sue Vickers shortly before she was murdered.

That year, 1978, the National Director suit for Seminar was purple and, as you can imagine, we were all having a difficult time finding shoes to match. Well, after weeks of fruitless shopping I finally stumbled upon a brand with the perfect material and color at a mall near my house in suburban Dallas. Naturally I called Sue, whom I had personally encouraged to move to Dallas a few months earlier, and told her about my discovery so that she too could buy a pair before they were all gone. Little did I know when we hung up that I would be the last person in Mary Kay to talk to Sue Vickers alive.

Sue did indeed go to the mall I had suggested and, as best the police could put the story together, was abducted as she was leaving by two men who robbed and murdered her. I, like everyone else, was devastated but with the additional burden of feeling I was responsible for her death. I could not escape the idea that if I had not called and told Sue to go to that particular mall on that particular day, she would still be alive. It was a heavy burden that I felt I might never shake until one day Mary Kay sat me down in her office and explained to me in no uncertain terms that Sue's death was not my fault. She had a way of communicating that made you believe. When Mary Kay focused her full attention on you, you felt that you were getting a message meant for no one else in the world and that there could be no question it was the gospel truth. From that day forward I began to let go, a little bit at a time, of the guilt I carried over Sue's death, though I still struggled with the senselessness of it all.

> ... as best the police could put the story together, [Sue] was abducted as she was leaving by two men who robbed and murdered her.

Anyone associated with Mary Kay has heard about the Miss Go-Give award, an honor bestowed on one woman in the Mary Kay sales force at each Seminar who has so consistently given of herself to others that she inspires and encourages everyone with whom she comes into contact. Well, you may be surprised to learn that Sue Vickers was the original Miss Go-Give, the first to win this coveted award that has become a pillar of the Mary Kay culture. It represents the ideal that we are to give without thought of what we might get in return and that we should be willing to help anyone who needs it even if we receive no immediate benefit. Receiving such an award would be a source of great pride in any organization, but because the Go-Give tradition was so important to Mary Kay, it is considered to be the highest award bestowed on a member of the sales force. Receiving that award from Mary Kay Ash in 1973 will always rank as one of my favorite accolades.

> It represents the ideal that we are to give without thought of what we might get in return.

After Sue's death, Mary Kay dedicated the National Miss Go-Give award to honor her memory and to inspire others to emulate her selflessness and enthusiasm. Looking back now, I realize that Mary Kay found a way to turn tragedy into inspiration in a way that allows Sue to live on in the hearts of the Mary Kay community in a positive way. We will always feel a pang of loss at the thought that Sue's smiling face and boundless energy are lost to us in this life, but now we will remember her as the original Miss Go-Give, a positive inspiration to millions of women who never had the privilege of knowing her but are nonetheless inspired by her. That is the magic of Mary Kay. And the Sue Vickers story is the perfect example of true, or "healthy," positive thinking: acknowledging a tragedy and mourning the very real and painful

> . . . acknowledging a tragedy and mourning the very real and painful loss of a friend and colleague, but then finding a way to honor the person instead of the tragedy . . .

loss of a friend and colleague, but then finding a way to honor the person instead of the tragedy, to make her enduring legacy one of joy and inspiration, not loss and grief.

As for Mary Kay, anyone who thinks the company's emphasis on positive thinking means it turns a blind eye to the hardships of life need only stop by the offices (or nowadays the website) of the Mary Kay Foundation. Toward the end of my career, I had the privilege of serving as one of the original members of the Mary Kay Foundation Advisory Council. I will admit that going into the experience I thought I knew a thing or two about Mary Kay, Inc., and its values, but I soon learned that Mary Kay's generosity and unflagging commitment to helping women around the world were far more than I could have ever imagined.

The Mary Kay Ash Charitable Foundation was formally estab-

Receiving my NSD plaque in 1974.

lished with the mission of raising research funds for "cancers affecting women." In 2000, the foundation expanded the scope of its mission and now also works to "prevent violence against women." In 2009 the foundation shortened its name to the Mary Kay Foundation, but while the name may be smaller, the impact has only gotten larger as today the foundation raises and donates millions of dollars annually to help improve the lives of women.

> I had the privilege of serving as one of the original members of the Mary Kay Foundation Advisory Council.

Here then is the true legacy of Mary Kay and her philosophy: that by building a company that empowers and enables women to set their own course in life through hard work and "belief in ourselves," Mary Kay was able to create a vehicle, through the Mary Kay Foundation, that helps women and their families survive two of the most negative experiences facing women today: cancer and domestic violence. So, if someone asks me why I feel so positive about this company after all these years, I tell them it's because I know that women can make a difference for themselves and others when we work together and stay true to our values. I hope you feel the same.

6

A Single Mother's
Story of Survival

"Necessity is the mother of taking chances."
—MARK TWAIN

My personal belief is that the feminine side of leadership is Mary Kay's greatest gift to the world. She has been recognized, and rightly so, by the Wharton School of Business as one of the great leaders of our times. Harvard Business School has written several case studies on Mary Kay, and John P. Kotter, the Harvard professor who studies Mary Kay's leadership style, told *Fortune Magazine* that Mary Kay is "an opportunity generating machine" that does a great job of leaders creating leaders. And that's precisely the role Mary Kay implored her Independent National Sales Directors to take on.

Mildred Caldwell, successful
single mother.

I was fortunate enough to have been named one of those leaders in 1974, the fifth woman in the nation to attain the Independent National Sales Director title. Today there are more than five hundred NSDs leading a sales force of over two million, but I know that Mary Kay's values are still solidly in place in every one of them so that the "opportunity generating machine" continues to run like a top. I feel it is a real testament to the so-called female side of leadership that in the process of giving women a voice, Mary Kay would also rekindle the fire of love, kindness, and respect in the business world. She believed wholeheartedly in the Golden Rule, and this Biblical principle became instrumental in her leadership philosophy. She asked us to search our souls to find our "best self" and, once found, to share it with others so that we could bring more women along on this incredible journey. As with so many of Mary Kay's ideas, I wholly embraced the golden rule as a business principle. It cuts across all geographic, social, demographic, and cultural boundaries and, I believe, speaks especially to women as it offers the promise of "doing well by doing good," and that is, as they say, an offer we can't refuse.

> She asked us to search our souls to find our "best self" and, once found, to share it with others.

I believe that one of the reasons the Mary Kay business plan (used in conjunction with the Mary Kay value system of God first, family second, and career third) has been so successful is that it is flexible enough to help women improve their lives no matter what their initial circumstances. Put another way, it can meet you where you are. Take, for example, a consultant and single mom named Mildred Caldwell, who joined the Unit of my dear friend, three-time Million-Dollar Director (and the first Million-Dollar Director from the Dingler Area), and former annual Miss Go-Give award winner, Janice Hull, back in 1976. Now, I can tell you that trying to survive as a single mother of two girls in North Carolina in the late seventies was no small challenge. The cards were stacked against her, to say the least.

Janice Hull, three-time Million Dollar Director.

At the time she joined the company, Mildred was working full-time as a bank teller while also holding down two part-time jobs as a waitress and hostess. Obviously, these were jobs that required her to be physically present (i.e., away from her children) at a time when no one had heard of flex time. Sick kid? Parent–teacher conference? Tough. These were problems Mildred had to work out on her own if she wanted to keep the wolves at bay and provide for her family.

Then Mildred met Janice Hull, and everything began to change. Now, to really get to know Mildred you have to know that she is someone for whom faith was very important, and no one had to tell her to put God first, family second, and career third. She was way

> . . . not only can Mary Kay meet you where you are, it can take you where you . . . want to go and you can still enjoy the journey.

ahead of us on that score. It should therefore come as no surprise that Mildred had been praying in earnest for a solution to her dilemma of wanting to be a good mother while needing to provide for her family financially. Well, when Janice came into her life (specifically her bank) Mildred knew that this was the answer she had been seeking, and within forty-eight hours of their first meeting, Mildred had a promising new career, a new extended Mary Kay family, and a new Director to whom she would become like a sister over the next seventeen years.

If this was a Hollywood story, it would probably end with Mildred rising through the ranks and driving off into the sunset in a pink Cadillac as the No. 1 National Sales Director. But that isn't Mildred's story. Mildred's story shows that not only can Mary Kay meet you where you are, it can take you where you (as opposed to someone else) want to go and you can still enjoy the journey. Mildred left her glamorous life in the food service industry and became an outstanding Consultant. She put both of her daughters through college and then paid for both of their weddings before finally remarrying, on her own terms, years later. There is no doubt that Mildred is a success story, but it was success on her terms and in accordance with her values.

Sadly, Mildred died of cancer in May 1993 but not before qualifying for Queen's Court of Sales for that year's Seminar. Mary Kay herself called Mildred in the hospital to congratulate her and ask if there was anything she or the company could do to help, and that is the Mary Kay I knew and loved: the business icon who would stop and take the time to call one of her frontline salespeople to congratulate and comfort her during such a difficult time. At times like these, Mary Kay still feels like the intimate sorority I joined back in the sixties when we were just a group of (mostly) like-minded women trying to help each other overcome life's obstacles while taking advantage of a wonderful opportunity.

> Mildred didn't start her business to get rich or for celebrity; she did it to help her family.

Like Mary Kay herself, Mildred didn't start her business to get rich or for celebrity; she did it to help her family. Mary Kay started this business to help women just like Mildred who wanted to take care of their families on their own terms. Mildred's daughters have vivid memories of their mother doing extra shows whenever she had to pay an unexpected bill or to buy something they needed. Whenever a need arose, Mildred would simply "work her Mary Kay" until it was met. Of course, her fellow Unit members also became a second family for her and an important source of emotional support when her health began to fail. On several occasions Mildred told Janice, "Mary Kay is my life," and so many of us can relate to that statement.

> She wanted to design a business that any woman, in any situation (and ultimately in any country), could use to better herself and her family while still staying loyal to her values.

Mildred recruited six people during her all-too-brief Mary Kay career, and it wasn't so that she could qualify to become a Director or to increase her income. Mildred simply wanted to share with other women what she truly believed God had placed in her life, so that they could have the same opportunity she had been given. And that, I believe, is the essence of what Mary Kay was trying to create when she founded her company. She wanted to design a business that any woman, in any situation (and ultimately in any country), could use to better herself and her family while still staying loyal to her values, and then share it with other women.

I think it may be something unique to women that really makes the Mary Kay business plan work. When we find something good, something beneficial to ourselves and our families, we want to share it, to "pay it forward," as they say and help other women we think would benefit from what we've discovered. Today there are millions of Mildreds around the world "working their Mary Kay," improving their lives, enjoying their extended Mary Kay family, and sharing this amazing opportunity with other women. Just like Mary Kay intended.

7

Mary Kay's Global Impact

"If you would know the road ahead,
ask someone who has traveled it."
—CHINESE PROVERB

My son, second only to my husband in sharing this life-altering experience with me, had a front-row view watching and encouraging me in my business. As he's kept up with Mary Kay's progress in world markets, Devin has observed that many of the views in this country in the 1960s would be analogous to some of the foreign countries of today, where women have learned about free enterprise from Mary Kay and welcomed the chance to better the lives of their families. I saw this myself when a magazine in the Czech Republic followed some Czech women attending Seminar in Dallas one of the years I ranked number one in the sales force. The reporter traveling with them highlighted a visit the Czech women made to my home. The author listed my accolades and took pains to describe our lifestyle: "To pass the main gates (to our home) felt like being in a Hollywood film." She

> "To pass the main gates (to our home) felt like being in a Hollywood film."

shared my advice on such "high-level" business secrets as how to succeed in a happy marriage! (How? You need separate bathrooms and televisions!) Asked how to succeed in a career, I said, "Your biggest need is your will to succeed." More than the lifestyle, however, it was classic Mary Kay principles that these women of a different culture and generation wanted to know more about. It goes without saying that they loved our products; what they wanted to hear from me was more Mary Kay stories, additional lessons from my success, and lots of advice on how to weave this business into the fabric of their lives, their families, and their communities (*see original article and translation in this chapter*).

Barbara Sunden
Current No. 1 NSD

I recently compared notes on this subject with the current No. 1 Independent National Sales Director in Mary Kay. She is a leader whose global Area finds her working throughout the world and, I am proud to say, she's one of the Dingler Area's original offspring: the beautiful Barbara Sunden. She sees firsthand this same phenomenon today as she travels, teaches, and speaks to women in Asia, South America, and Europe. "Women across the world love the *connection* with Mary Kay the woman," Barbara says. "Helping women find their own talents is a concept that no one does better than the Mary Kay training." I would like to add that women across the world also love the connection with Barbara Sunden who, like Mary Kay, is helping women realize their lifelong dreams.

All this makes me realize how simple it is to understand Mary Kay's global impact in the twenty-first century. To understand how women in so many emerging economies around the world relate to—or rather, clamor for—our "pioneer" stories is to understand the key to much of the Mary Kay business success that has arisen from one woman's dream in 1963 (coincidentally, this was shortly after the president created the Presidential Commission on the Status of Women). We understood that Mary Kay's mission was founded on respect and admiration for women, on treating others the way you'd like to be treated. I cannot think of any place on earth this wouldn't work. The vision was to motivate and to raise the status

> . . . women in so many emerging economies around the world relate to—or rather clamor for—our 'pioneer' stories . . .

of women and thereby create a legacy that could be perpetuated *by* women. When Mary Kay clearly laid out a ladder of success for women, that was in itself an invaluable tool for those of us accustomed to the old boys' network and the unspoken code for succeeding in a male-dominated corporate culture. We were aware as leaders of the Mary Kay sales force that it was our responsibility to find our own strengths, reach out to other women, and then bring them along with us. Women across the world today find their collective voices in the same way we did. Mary Kay defines a philosophical movement, one that empowers women and provides insight into a new kind of leadership—the female kind.

> Millenials laugh in disbelief when I mention that in the 1960s, classified ads were segregated by sex . . .

If I seem to harp on this, it's because I want to be crystal clear about how significant it is that when Mary Kay came along, there were no role models for businesswomen. Millennials laugh in disbelief when I mention that in the 1960s, classified ads were segregated by sex; magazine articles for women focused on baking, cleaning, etc. You need look no further for an example than the hit television series *Mad Men,* set in the 1960s. When the producer/creator of *Mad Men* was chastised recently for keeping its women characters in the background, he defended this as an accurate portrayal of women in the workforce of the 1960s. Women knew their place in corporate America: they didn't have one. Business conversations among the women of *Mad Men* are not part of the show's dialogue because, as its producer stated, women simply didn't have a place. You've probably heard the statement "A woman's place is in the home." Mary Kay Ash loved taking that line and adding that a woman's place is indeed in the House, also in the Senate, and in the boardroom as well.

> A woman's place is indeed in the House, also in the Senate, and in the boardroom as well.

By the mid-1970s, when Mary Kay Inc. became a publicly traded company, Mary Kay Ash was reportedly the first female chair of a company traded on the New York Stock Exchange. But that's not at all what her sales force leaders loved most about her. We coveted our relationships with Mary Kay, her personal wisdom, and how she role modeled leadership, so much so in the early days of the company that we flew to Dallas from all over the country for Sales Director meetings. It was this strong connection with our company founder that bonded us instantly and made us want to perpetuate what she began. Here, finally, was a leader we could relate to. We put her on a pedestal, but she remained as down-to-earth and practical a woman as I ever met. I remember that at those meetings the Sales Directors from Dallas brought in food for covered-dish luncheons so the meetings could continue uninterrupted. The food editor of the local newspaper wrote a story about this unconventional business meeting ritual, clamoring to publish our recipes and hear about our beauty secrets—and not a word about our business strategies. I'd venture that most people in Dallas didn't have a clue about the trailblazing going on in that building on Carpenter Freeway. By the way, the price for out-of-towners who couldn't bring a home-cooked dish was a dollar—quite a bargain for lunch as well as priceless time with our mentor. We were eager to soak in all the learning we possibly could, and fortunate indeed to be part of a culture that encouraged sharing that wisdom. We had finally found the role model our gender had been lacking.

> We had finally found the role model our gender had been lacking.

I may not have been able to articulate it, but I always felt my faith and my family should come before my work. I know personally how much I appreciated not having to choose between them. All working women understand the mercurial life most women experience, especially those with children. Women wear so many hats, yet Mary Kay made it patently clear that when family needs arose, those should come first. She urged us to establish and maintain our priorities, even going so far as to caution that if we didn't keep our priorities in order, we probably would not succeed. Or we might not succeed with our family intact. It was God first, family second, and career third, and "in that order it works." She implored us not to beat ourselves up over the fact that we had to put

> Mary Kay made it patently clear that when family needs arose, those should come first.

our business goals on hold when oftentimes in our mobile society we had to move our business as husbands got transferred. There are no territories in the Mary Kay model simply because Mary Kay knew firsthand the angst of having built a sales territory and then being forced to leave it behind and start over when she had to relocate. We knew she'd always be there urging us to reestablish our goals once we could get back on track. I can attest to this from firsthand experience when Bruce and I made the decision in 1976 to leave South Carolina: Mary Kay was there for us every step of the way. I remember shortly before Mary Kay suffered her debilitating stroke in 1996 how extremely proud she was to learn that in the month leading up to the close of the Seminar year, one of the Million Dollar Sales Directors had found time to teach Bible School at her church. Mary Kay called these kinds of decisions—both large and small ones—having your priorities in order!

Learn to Work with People Where They Are

Mary Kay was so attuned to the fact—especially in the sales field—that women always need to keep their batteries charged. She emphasized to us how important a Monday sales meeting was in that regard. Not only did we need to recharge those batteries and keep our team's enthusiasm high, but we also needed to counter any negativity the women might be getting about their Mary Kay business from friends and family. She liked the idea of a Monday meeting, when a Beauty Consultant was fresh off the weekend and might have been exposed to relatives or church friends prone to ridicule the idea of a direct sales business. And don't think women didn't have to deal with that kind of discouragement and disparagement. I remember a minister's wife among the early pioneers in the sales force who was afraid to let on she had a Mary Kay business lest some among

> . . . not only was it important that my Unit members attend their sales meetings . . . it was even more important that they never miss the annual Mary Kay Seminar.

her husband's congregation look askance. My own mother-in-law, proud as she was of what I'd accomplished, felt uncomfortable talking about my career around friends and family. She felt it just wasn't ladylike to discuss such matters.

Once I grasped the importance of Monday sales meetings, I

hosted two, one in the morning and one in the early evening. I came to understand that not only was it important that my Unit members attend their sales meetings where they could crow about the week's accomplishments in front of women who were cheering them on, but it was even more important that they never miss the annual Mary Kay Seminar. That, I would say, is where we get our big picture, where secure inside what we fondly called the Pink Bubble, we could bask unabashedly in our accomplishments. We could set our goals and resell ourselves on the dream. I found that I was able to focus more clearly on my goals once I'd been around people who were doing the same things I was doing and getting results. Hearing the speeches and "I Stories" of women who were succeeding and attending classes always helped me get to the next milestone in my career while nudging along my competitive streak. Soaking in all that positivism and encouragement was invigorating. One of my good friends once asked me in front of the entire audience at Seminar if I couldn't slow down my progress just a little so she could move into No. 1 from her No. 2 position since it was her last year before retirement! I have to admit I briefly thought about it, but quickly came to my senses.

> "Women learn more in the line at the restroom than they do in the classroom sometimes."

At these mostly female business gatherings, we relished the fact that Mary Kay required the Dallas Convention Center to turn all but a couple of the restrooms into women's rooms every Seminar. After all, our fearless founder opined, "Women learn more in the line at the restroom than they do in the classroom sometimes." To further hit home her point, she used to say there's as much learning in the hotel hallways at night as there ever is from the podium. Whether we were exchanging makeup tips or business tactics, that was a fact. While Mary Kay might be flippantly described as a "sorority" of sorts because of all the high-energy enthusiasm and hugs, there was sound strategy in creating that sort of environment. There was a great deal of learning and tons of motivation amid all the merriment. Truth be told, we were like sisters. There was community, a bond we shared. This was especially the case for those first ten or so of us to truly become successful in the business, yet a great deal of this sisterhood element remains even as the sales force count exceeds two million.

Because this is something so few can relate firsthand, I think it's important to talk about "how it was" when we charter members of Mary Kay's Top Ten National Sales Directors were together. It shaped who we were. We traveled like a privileged band of sisters, and our husbands traveled along with us. We shared nearly everything, including our problems, and I can recall many discussions that lasted well into the night. Mary Kay Ash traveled with us like one of the gang, yet we always kept her on a pedestal and always appreciated the way she kept that edge of leadership in her dealings with us.

> Mary Kay Ash traveled with us like one of the gang, yet we always kept her on a pedestal and always appreciated the way she kept that edge of leadership . . .

Mary Kay, as friendly and warmhearted as always, figured out how to keep the appropriate distance of leadership as she closely mentored those of us who were the original sales force leaders. She encouraged us to pay close attention because she already knew what we were to find out: it's hard for leaders to become "best friends" with those they lead. The company once published a book that related my experience with Mary Kay's wonderful humor and how she was able to bring levity to situations. Once, seated beside her at a fancy dinner with thousands of adoring and admiring fans looking on, Mary Kay whispered a hilarious comment and then kept her cool as I exploded with laughter. She demurely took a sip of her water, never losing her regal composure while I was doubled over with laughter. Another time she grabbed an extra dessert from the head table, telling me she needed two so she could have one for each cheek, and she was not referring to the cheeks to which you apply rouge! Finding herself frequently at banquets and head tables, she became quite adept at pulling out a little shaker of jalapeño powder from her purse and discreetly spicing up the bland food being served. At other times, following some fancy banquet when she'd had hardly enough time to even eat the meal served in her honor, she'd ask her driver to pull through a fast food restaurant on the way home or to her hotel.

Dress as if You're About to Run into Your Husband's Former Girlfriend

Mary Kay got our attention with a request any woman would instantly grasp, and that is that even if you're going to the grocery store, dress as if you're about to run into your husband's former girlfriend! Mary Kay took such great pains to be sure that we knew the importance of keeping up our own image, and that without fail we always looked the part of leaders. These intangibles are, I believe, what differentiates the Mary Kay sales force. The professional demeanor and well-groomed image of these women certainly contribute to the indelible Mary Kay brand image. Even in her later years, Mary Kay reputedly never left the office without first applying a fresh coat of lipstick. She told us in the early days that if we could only afford one dress, to make sure it flattered our figure and to wear it every time we had an important

> Mary Kay reputedly never left the office without first applying a fresh coat of lipstick.

occasion. She wanted us to always be well groomed because, as she stressed, other women are looking to us as role models. She also urged us to get a wig and/or a turban to wear on those bad hair days. I was interested to read recently that (another) famous cosmetics company funded research on the negative psychological implications of the so-called "bad hair day" and smiled to myself that Mary Kay knew instinctively what that company probably spent millions to "discover."

Putting Professionalism on a Higher Level

One time when several of us were in the lobby of a hotel in South Carolina, we couldn't help but notice the admiring glances of the men who were in the hotel for conventions, meetings, or just a business lunch. All of us were impeccably coiffed and dressed in the beautiful matching tailored business suits worn by the Sales Directors that year. We couldn't help but notice the irony and joked among ourselves that whatever it was these men *thought* we were doing in that hotel, we were quite confident they figured we were "professionals" at it! None of these men could have imagined, we giggled, that not only were our businesses likely earning more than theirs, but we were having way more fun in the process by poking holes in their conventional female stereotypes. More important, we were working to establish the idea that a professional businesswoman need not dress, act, or talk like a man to be successful.

> A professional businesswoman need not dress, act, or talk like a man to be successful.

Another leadership tip I picked up along the way was that, wearing skirts as we did, we knew without a doubt that our hose should *never* have runs or snags. Panty hose came into being the same decade we did, and yes, we wore them almost every waking hour until Mary Kay relaxed the sales force dress code to allow open-toed pumps, bare legs, and, at the appropriate time in the twenty-first century, even trousers at non-company functions. Before that, we were advised to always keep a spare pair in the glove box of our car, and at Company events, at least those where National Sales Directors were in attendance, a stash of pantyhose was always kept on hand for "emergencies" (i.e., runs). While we didn't have the burden of paparazzi following and photographing our every move as celebrities do today, we always were aware people could be watching. This hit home for me recently when I was checking into a resort and the clerk at the front desk, after reading my name, got a little excited because she was a newly minted Mary Kay Beauty Consultant. The first thing I did, out of sheer habit, was to think about what my hair looked like after traveling all day. Because I wanted her to have that good first impression, I hastily explained to this total stranger that I had a spa and hair appointment that afternoon, which thankfully I did. Several years retired and those old habits still die hard.

We also learned from our leader to take care of ourselves. For me that meant that on Monday, in order to gracefully make it through the day when I had both a morning and an evening sales meeting, I needed a long soak in the tub in between. We joke that my son thought all moms took such long baths every Monday. I think Devin also thought all moms had an office at home and that lots of them drove pink Cadillacs.

> Devin also thought all moms had an office at home and that lots of them drove pink Cadillacs.

The first year Mary Kay awarded *five* pink Cadillacs was 1969. I had been a Sales Director only eight months and hadn't completed a full year's contest period—though I still ranked number eight nationally—so I didn't get one of the initial fleet. I told myself that I never really cared that much about the car. I also wasn't in that initial group named to the National Sales Director position in 1971 because I was having a terrific time being a highly successful Sales Director in South Carolina. However, soon after the position was created, I saw the pink car Helen McVoy had earned as a National Sales Director (it was an upgrade from the ones available to Sales Directors) and called our vice president of sales to find out what I needed to do to get one like hers. I learned that the cars like Helen's were only for National Sales Directors. Well, there went that competitive streak again, and it wasn't long before I debuted as a National Sales Director (in 1974), fully committed to having one of those cars and whatever other perks came along with the NSD position.

> There was definitely a protocol for how we treated those pink Cadillacs. 'I've never seen a dirty pink Cadillac,' Mary Kay said, 'and I hope I never do.'

There was definitely a protocol for how we treated those pink Cadillacs. "I've never seen a dirty pink Cadillac," Mary Kay said, "and I hope I never do." I took that a step further, making sure that as we all began to spend more time in our cars, Mary Kay career car drivers were mindful that Beauty Consultants and customers alike love to peek inside these coveted symbols of success, so they

Receiving the keys to my first pink Cadillac.

should be neat and not filled with fast-food wrappers, curlers, or other clutter. I constantly emphasized that if every Consultant in your Unit is not either consciously or subconsciously after your job (and your car), then you aren't selling them on the dream.

This Business Is Between Your Ears

With an increasingly large group in my Area, I knew I had to work out how I was going to reach and teach all of them effectively. I learned I was most effective if I worked with a limited number at a time. Family was important, and so I had to learn to be firm in the decision I made that I couldn't travel all week to develop my Area. When one Sales Director asked why I didn't fly in more often to visit her city, I explained, "If I did what you're asking for, then none of you would want my job." I did keep in constant contact with them, calling them when I thought there was a goal on the horizon they should go for. I talked to their husbands sometimes if I thought that would help get the man in the family on *her* side! Mary

> . . . I occasionally hosted special events for husbands to attend . . .

Kay had, after all, taught us that the way to be most successful was to share our job and goals with others. To keep the desire going, I occasionally hosted special events for husbands to attend—covered-dish suppers, for example—to enlighten them on their wives' new endeavors. My own husband tells me that he couldn't believe I was so goal oriented when it came to working with my Unit and Area. He always noticed, he said, that one of my strong suits was checking the level of commitment of my team, and I knew that family support was critical to them. He knew how proud I was of one personal statistic—that of the high proportion of Dingler Area Beauty Consultants who eventually became Sales Directors. That's the classic Mary Kay growth curve, but it doesn't just magically happen. It's one of the things I worked at constantly. Women in my Unit and Area also knew that if they didn't hear from me very often, it was perhaps because it didn't appear that they were interested in working harder or committed to a new goal.

One evening we had twenty guests at our sales meeting, many of them very interested in exploring this business opportunity. Among them was one very stylish, sophisticated woman who voiced loudly that she wasn't sure she would ever be interested in a Mary Kay business. Knowing that one negative comment can poison 80 percent of those listening, I kindly but firmly hastened to inform her that everyone who wishes to doesn't automatically make the cut as a Beauty Consultant. The person who sponsors them into the Company has to feel they'd be good at this and that the timing's right. And it is true Mary Kay had often cautioned us to share this opportunity with the caliber of woman we wouldn't mind sharing a room with at Seminar. But that evening I could feel this woman's negativity sucking lots of the usual buoyancy out of the meeting, so I went out on a limb by telling the woman, "Well, I'm not sure you'd be accepted even if you applied." She was the first to sign her Beauty Consultant agreement that evening. It's also true that sometimes it's the least likely women who turn out to be most likely to succeed later.

> Mary Kay had often cautioned us to share this opportunity with the caliber of woman we wouldn't mind sharing a room with at Seminar

The business itself isn't complicated, even though people tend to want to make it more difficult than it is. I remember when it clicked for me, when I realized that we really were changing people's lives and I began to experience a new level of enjoyment. My favorite part of the job was seeing women succeed and hearing about what they'd been able to do for their kids, aging parents, or husbands stuck in jobs they hated, how they'd been able to make a difference in their communities. I saw that earning a little more money could make a lot happen in people's lives, and it became my focus to show women how a Mary Kay business can be a money-making proposition. From my experience of having to get Bruce to co-sign my first business loan, I became very good at getting bankers in South Carolina to understand that the investment these women were making in their Mary Kay businesses could reap great rewards for their bank. Again that was advice straight from Mary Kay, but I used it successfully with a local banker. Our banking relationship had developed late one afternoon when, in a panic, I called a Greenville telephone operator to see if she knew of a bank that stayed open past the usual 3:00 p.m. closing time (remember, this was 1968, before instantaneous monetary transactions, and this particular month I needed to get the paperwork and a cashier's check for one of my recruits in the mail by day's end, and I was racing to make it). Turns out, she did know of a new bank that was open until 5:00 p.m., so I called with an impassioned plea that they do me a huge favor: issue a $100 cashier's check today!

> I saw that earning a little more money could make a lot happen in people's lives

"Would you please stay open five minutes past five?" I pleaded while I quickly smeared on my lipstick. When they said yes, I got the teenager next door to go with me and stay with Devin in the car while I ran into the bank. The bank president himself had stayed after hours. He told me he wanted to meet the person who had more enthusiasm in her voice than he usually heard. As you may have guessed, he issued the check and it arrived in Dallas on time. I knew from that experience that once he saw what a small loan could do for a Mary Kay business, he would be on board as a friendly banker. Later, we persuaded at least one husband to move his business account to that bank, and before too long they had fifty different and new Mary Kay business accounts. In that 2001 newspaper interview I mentioned earlier, I'm quoted on how Mary Kay had taken women who couldn't even *sign* for a loan at a bank and turned them into women who now have the privilege to *own* banks.

TWO YEARS IN THIS BUSINESS IS LIKE A DEGREE IN PSYCHOLOGY AND FOUR YEARS . . . A PH.D.

Mary Kay used to tell us that the greatest Beauty Consultant, the best Sales Director, and the smartest National Sales Director has yet to be born, and I really do believe that. I never thought I was the smartest woman in the room and I learned early on not to believe in my own press because I believe it's so important to stay grounded. At Mary Kay's urging, we were realistic about the fact that we weren't expected to be great at everything. We grasped immediately the concept of surrounding ourselves with those who are good at what we weren't. We also mas-

> I learned early on not to believe in my own press . . . it's so important to stay grounded.

tered the art of delegating and sharing resources. We were, in essence, the quintessential "millionaires next door," often running our business from our kitchen table and largely without most people even knowing what it was that we did.

Coaching and mentoring became my key strength as a leader. I learned from Mary Kay the importance of providing incentives to women, something they felt they couldn't do without (remember how I couldn't do without that particular pink Cadillac?). I also learned that women aren't motivated solely by money (though it often helps). The ability to read people, to size up situations from intuitive observations, and to be clear about the "big" picture we were painting as a Unit—these were some of the areas where I felt I did have something to offer. As Mary Kay leaders, we were often working with women I wouldn't exactly call "ambitious." More often than not, they could best be described as "very insecure." We learned to motivate women until they believed they could achieve great things, and we had to understand that not everyone was as motivated or as driven as we might be. Often we had to first convince a woman she could succeed and then show and prove to her that doing it wasn't "scary." I once took a promising potential team member to a class where no one showed up and another one to a class that was full but where no one bought anything! It's easy to kill people's motivation before they believe they can soar. In my own Area, we would start with baby steps. First, we'd help show a new Beauty Consultant how to book her initial appointments and how to schedule those first classes to begin to establish a customer base. Only when she'd started holding skin care classes could she begin to see who might want to learn more about the product and the opportunity. We intentionally brought people along at a slower pace, encouraging them not to talk about the next step or the next goal until they'd mastered the previous one. Pretty soon the goals and the rewards were growing into cars and trips and dreams come true.

By the same token, there is no sense in trying to talk someone into something they don't really want. I had to learn that working with people where they want to be is far better (and significantly less frustrating) than trying to make them

> Women aren't motivated solely by money (though it often helps).

> I once took a promising potential team member to a class where no one showed up . . .

into another me. Everyone didn't want what I had attained, and that had to be okay. The success syndrome causes some women to sabotage their own efforts any time they get close to attaining their goal. Other times they get help. I remember one husband who, every time his wife was close to earning a Mary Kay car, would take her on an exciting trip for a couple of weeks. He effectively took

> In that era, some husbands could be quite threatened by their wives' success.

her away from her business at precisely the point she otherwise would have qualified for the car (in that era, some husbands could be quite threatened by their wives' success). As Sales Directors, especially in the early days, when we traveled we generally stayed in the homes of the team members we visited. I learned so much seeing women in their home environment, watching them interact with their families. It helped me to focus on those with whom I needed to spend the most time. Mary Kay used to say that two years in this business was like a degree in psychology and four years . . . a Ph.D.

One year onstage at Seminar, Mary Kay congratulated me for attaining a new level in the multimillion-dollar club. I said to her that day—and I still feel this way—that I was so busy having fun and changing lives that the millions just happened. All of a sudden one day I looked back and saw nineteen brilliant women who had become National Sales Directors out of my Area, and it was one of my proudest moments. I felt I had managed to make a real contribution to Mary Kay's sterling legacy of women leaders. Even more wonderful is the knowledge that this legacy will continue to grow long after I'm gone.

With Mary Kay at my NSD debut.

Tour of our Dallas home by Mary Kay Consultants and Directors who contributed to the Dingler Area becoming No. 1 Worldwide.

EXECUTIVE NATIONAL SALES DIRECTOR
DORETHA DINGLER

Dallas, Texas

Czech Republic

patří k špičce Mary Kay – není ocenění, ktere by nezískaľ.
vychovala 18 National Sales Directors v USA, Kanadě a Mexiku.

Měla jsem to obrovské štěstí, že jsem se při své poslední cestě do Dallasu v listopadu loňského roku s Dorethy sešla osobně. Pozvala mé do svého domu a z naplánovaných 30ti minut byly téměř tři hodiny. Čas utíkal jako voda a já doslova hltala každé slovo, každičký pohyb této živé legendy Mary Kay. Doretha je velmi přirozená, milá, ale i přesto mi bylo jasné, že přede mnou stojí Někdo.

V roce 1965 byla pozvána na seminář a smlouvu podepsala, protože neměla co dělat, vytoužené děťátko stále nepřicházelo, manžel trávil cele dny v kanceláři. Neuplynuly ani dva měsíce a Doretha zjistila, že je konečně těhotná. Malý Devin dostal ve všem přednost a kufřík letěl na dno skříně.

Současně s přestěhováním rodiny do státu Jižní Karolína obdržela kosmetická poradkyně Doretha Dingler dopis, který ji informoval, že byla vyřazena ze systému – tj. terminována. Tento list papíru se stal oním památným výstřelem, který nastartoval jednu z nejzářivějších

kariér ve společnosti Mary Kay. Během pouhých šesti měsíců se Doretha stala Sales Director a její tým se ocitl mezi těmi nejlepšími.

A z výsluní slávy a úspěchu nikdy neodešla ani ona, ani její tým a v posledních letech ani její národní oblast.

Doretha „vyrůstala" vedle Mary Kay Ash, která byla její učitelkou a kamarádkou zároveň. Ona ji naučila to prostě: „Jestliže něco opravdu moc chceš, pak najdeš či vytvoříš způsob, jak toho dosáhnout."

„Je to tak prosté, nehledejte za tím nic složitého. Je třeba mít jen správný přístup, vědět, že naše podnikání je o lidech, mít je ráda a jde to samo." To mi Doretha říkala, když jsem s obdivem fotografovala její obyvací salón. „Víte, měly jsme jen pět barev podkladových bází a ještě k tomu nás nikdo neučil, jak je správně používat. Někdy z toho byla legrace, jindy trapas, ale my zkrátka semináře milovaly. A pak jednoho dne Sue (Sue Vickers, Sales Director, která byla zákeřně zavražděna ve věku 30 let. Mary Kay na její počest vytvořila zvláštní a nejprestižnější ocenění společnosti – MISS Go – Give.) vymyslela tzv. ACAPULCO LOOK (Acapulco vzhled), který spočíval ve smíchání dvou odstinů. Úspěchy jsme s tím slavily dalších pět let!"

Dorotha patří k milionářkám Mary Kay, za 37 let u společnosti vydělala na provizích více než 6 miliónů dolarů, byla třetí National Sales Director v Mary Kay. Vyhrála všechny zájezdy pro TOP NSD a jak se

NATIONAL SALES DIRECTOR 27

mi svěřila, v životě si s manželem nekoupili dovolenou. S úsměvem

si posteskla, že poslední 2 roky už moc nejezdí, protože už byli -

samozřejmě s Mary Kay - po celém světě. V září loňského roku

ohromila celou společnost výše její měsíční provize: 148 000 dola-

rů – absolutní rekord v celé historii Mary Kay. V lednu 2003 odešla

Executive National Sales Director Doretha Dingler do „důchodu

MK" a získala status EMERITUS. Bude se plně věnovat manželovi

Bruceovi, který je po operaci srdce. Syn vystudoval práva a nyní

studuje finance, snacha je bytovou architektkou a pomohla zařídit

tchánům jejich luxusní dům v prestižní vilové čtvrti v Dallasu (projekt

bránou bylo jako z hollywoodského filmu a zbytek nebyl o nic

„horší"). Po 32 letech řízení růžového cadillacu si nyní Doretha

vybrala stříbrné BMW.

Závěrem mi prozradila, jak mít i po 40 letech šťastné manželství:

potřebujete k tomu dvě koupelny a dva televizory!

„Víte, neexistuje žádné kouzelné zaklínadlo k úspěchu, neexistují

žádné hranice. Musíte jen chtít. Přeji vašim Directorkám a porad-

kyním hodně štěstí." Rozloučila se se mnou žena, která pomáhala

psát paní Mary Kay Ash dějiny jedné z nejúžasnějších společností,

jejíž součástí máte čest být i VY!

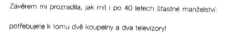

1 malovaný portrét NSD Dorethy Dingler –
  první NSD byly portrétovány, nikoli foceny
2 na návštěvě u Dorethy Dingler: zprava Elga Desautel
  (trenérka pro Evropu), NSD Doretha Dingler, Kateřina
  Braithwaite (trenérka pro ČR a SR)
3 Večeře manželů Dinglerových s vnukem p. Mary Kay Ash
  Ryanem
4 vánoční gratulace manželů Dorethy a Bruce Dinglerových,
  kterou posílali své NSD oblasti
5 Doretha v části svého obývacího pokoje v luxusním domě
  v prestižní Dallaské čtvrti – tak žije NSD
6 malý pohled do soukromí – šatna Dorethy

Translation of previous article

EXECUTIVE NATIONAL SALES DIRECTOR DORETHA DINGLER

I was very lucky, that on my latest trip to Dallas, in November 2002, I had a chance to meet personally Mrs. Doretha Dingler. She invited me to her home and instead of 30 minutes, as we planned, we spent together almost 3 hours. Time went by quickly and I was patiently listening to every word she said and watching every move, this live legend of Mary Kay made. Doretha is a very natural and pleasant woman, but it was clear to me, that there's not just anybody standing in front of me.

In 1965, when she desired for a child so much and her husband spent most of the time in his office, she was invited to Mary Kay skin care class and signed the contract. But in two months she finally found out she was pregnant and so the showcase ended up at the bottom of her closet, because little Devin received all of the priorities and attention.

Along with the family move to South Carolina, beauty consultant Doretha Dingler received a letter, which informed her, that she was about to be terminated in Mary Kay. And that letter became the memorable moment, which started one of the most brilliant careers in Mary Kay ever. During only six months time, Doretha became Sales Director and her team found themselves among the best ones. Since then, Doretha and her team, never left the peak of glory and success.

Doretha grew up next to Mary Kay Ash, who had been her teacher and friend, who taught her, "If you want something very much, then you will find, or create the way, how to reach your goal."

"It is so simple, do not look at it as something difficult. All you need is the right attitude and knowing, that our business is about people, about loving them and that is just the way it works." That is what Doretha told me, while I was taking pictures of her living room. "Did you know, we had only five colors of coverage foundations and nobody ever taught us how to use them? Sometimes it was fun, but sometimes it was embarrassing, but despite that we all loved the skin care classes. And then one day, Sue invented ACAPULCO LOOK, which was based on mixing the two of the 5 shades. We benefited from that for another five years!" (Sue Vickers, Sales Director, who was brutally murdered at the age of 30. Mary Kay founded on her behalf special and the most prestigious award of the company: MISS GO-GIVE).

Doretha belongs to the millionaires of Mary Kay and during her working for 38 years at Mary Kay, she earned more than 10 million dollars on the commissions, she was the fifth National Sales Director in Mary Kay. She won all of the trips organized for TOP NSD and, as she confessed to me, that neither she nor her husband have ever bought a vacation. Doretha though "complained" a little bit, with the smile on her face, that for the past two years she has not been traveling a lot, because she already has traveled all over the world with Mary Kay. In September 2002, her monthly commission was 104,000 dollars, which is an absolute record in whole Mary Kay history. In January 2003, Doretha Dingler retired from MK and received status EMERITUS. Now she fully devoted herself to her husband and family. Their son graduated from law school and now is studying finances; their daughter-in-law is an interior designer and she is the one, who helped her parents-in-law to furnish their luxury house in a prestigious district of Dallas (to pas the main gates, felt like being in the Hollywood film and the rest was just as beautiful). After 32 years of driving the pink Cadillac, Doretha has chosen the silver BMW now.

At the end of my visit, she advised me, how to succeed in a happy marriage even after 45 years; you just need two bathrooms and two televisions!

"You know, there's no such miracle spell to the success, but there are no limits to it too. All you need is your will. I wish to all your Directors and your Beauty Consultants good luck." And then I said good-bye to the woman, who helped Mrs. Mary Kay to write the history of the most amazing company in the world and YOU are honored to be part of it too!

Pictures:
1. Painted portrait of NSD Doretha Dingler – first of NSD's were painted, not photographed.
2. Visiting at Doretha's home; from the right Elga Desautel(European trainer), NSD Doretha Dingler, Katerina Braithwaite (CR and SR trainer).
3. Dinner of Mr. and Mrs. Dingler with Mrs. Mary Kay's grandson, Ryan
4. Christmas greeting from Doretha and Bruce Dingler, which they were sending to their NSD field.
5. Doretha in her luxury living room – that is the way NSD lives
6. A little glance into her privacy – Doretha's dressing room.

8

Hurricanes, Terrorists, and Hijackers . . . Oh My!

*"We are each of us angels with only one wing,
we can only fly by embracing one another."*

—LUCRETIUS

I've already used the word *I* far more in this book than I'm comfortable with, simply because I couldn't figure out any other way to tell *my* story! In telling it, however, I could never forget to pay homage to the women who mentored me and those I was privileged to mentor. It illustrates one of the greatest lessons ever taught to me by Mary Kay, which is that we are raised up by virtue of those we help. She believed and said often that "giving" becomes a way of life. She supported wholeheartedly the idea that when we succeed we should always acknowledge and remember those who helped us along the way. It's true that in a commission model like Mary Kay's, compensation is linked and affected by the people with whom you share your success. In the Mary Kay marketing plan, the more people you help, the better off you become. But having reached and far exceeded that point, I can

> . . . there comes a time when it becomes about so much more than money.

honestly say there comes a time when it becomes about so much more than money. It becomes about changing lives.

And so it was for me. As I began to see lives changed for the better among those I had mentored, there was such an overwhelming feeling of satisfaction and pride. We always called it the "paycheck of the heart," and in that area I am rich beyond measure. It is amazing the twists and turns that led me onto the paths of so many wonderful women, and that's exactly the way Mary Kay always imagined it would be in her "dream" company.

> When we succeed we should always acknowledge and remember those who helped us along the way.

So, back to *my* story. . . .

Let me start with those who mentored me. We were referred to as charter members of the Top Ten, a prestigious group that came to be known as the Inner Circle. All of us were fiercely competitive, but even so there was a camaraderie among us that grew out of doing something so rare. Mary Kay reminded us frequently that we were making strides that few women in the business world had ever made. More than anything she wanted us, rather than competing with each other, to compete with ourselves and work to best our latest achievements. Well we certainly did that, but as we individually set the bar higher and higher for ourselves, we kind of nudged each other along. I remember one year when Mary Kay's son Richard told us there would come a day when Mary Kay's top saleswomen would earn the astounding sum of $10,000 a month. At the time most of us couldn't even imagine such a feat, but, as it happened, I exceeded that projection by a factor of ten when I broke the company record for highest-ever monthly commission check of $104,000.

> . . . I broke the company record for highest-ever monthly commission check of $104,000.

I always loved how the Mary Kay marketing plan allowed for that kind of staggering growth. We were encouraged as we moved up to get one foot firmly planted on each rung of the ladder just long enough to propel ourselves to the next higher rung. The career ladder was designed so there was always a next step, and believing we could achieve it was ingrained in us from day one.

Among the National Sales Directors, there were no cookie-cutter personalities or any one formula to ensure success. Each of us was unique in the way we chose to grow. We had typical girl-friend ties, and—as with that speech Mary Kay asked me to give my first year as a Sales Director—we were encouraged to share our secrets of success. And, yes, we certainly shared all manner of growing pains. We were all in the same boat after all, both in a figurative sense as well as, sometimes, literally. I mention this because there was one particular Top Ten trip we took with our husbands that sealed our bond once and for all and that took place, as it happens, on a boat.

> . . . in nearby waters earlier that day . . . [t]he *Achille Lauro,* an Italian cruise ship, had been hijacked

It was 1985, and our glorious annual Top Ten trip found us luxuriating on the *Stella Solaris* cruise ship. Early into the week's Mediterranean cruise we were urgently called together to hear some excruciating news: the horror of what had taken place in nearby waters earlier that day. The *Achille Lauro,* an Italian cruise ship, had been hijacked en route from Alexandria to Port Said, Egypt. It was an extremely tragic event, including the unimaginably brutal murder of a wheelchair-bound American passenger (you may have seen the movie that was later made of this terrible event—*The Hijacking of the Achille Lauro*). Along with this news, we were told that the terrorists were holding 438 hostages. I remember several of us gathered after the briefing and collectively decided we needed to get home as soon as possible. We planned to let Mary Kay Ash know our wishes to abandon the ship immediately. Before we could go to her, however, Mary Kay came to us. She announced that the staff had already arranged transportation in small planes that would get us to Athens, Greece, where any of us who wished to get out fast could fly home. The next words out of her mouth stunned everyone.

> Not one of us got off that ship. If Mary Kay Ash was going on, we were going on with her.

"We will continue this trip for those who wish to remain. I will be staying on the ship." There was stunned silence. Not one of us got off that ship. If Mary Kay Ash was going on, we were going on with her. We knew we were not out of danger and were unsure what would happen next—especially knowing that in the context of these anti-American acts of terror we were sailing with a legendary American icon. The captain advised that our ship was being immediately diverted to Egypt to escape being potential targets of Palestine Liberation Front hijackers. Few of us slept much, but sure enough when daylight dawned, there we were—the *Stella Solaris* was safely docked in Port Said, Egypt. The reality of what had happened hit home, however, when outside of our windows we saw the ship docked immediately adjacent to ours: the *Achille Lauro,* whose fifty-two-hour ordeal had ended when the hijackers surrendered. How close we came to potential disaster, we could only surmise; how brave our founder—of that we were positive—

With Mary
Kay and
the Captain
aboard the
Stella Solaris.

and none of us took our freedom for granted after that, I can assure you.

I couldn't help but think about how concerned my mother was about this particular trip given the unrest in the Middle East and the fact that I had assured her that terrorists don't hijack ships, they hijack planes, and we would be on a ship for the majority of this trip. Of course, after hearing on the news that a ship had been hijacked close to the same waters we were in, and having no cell phones at that time to let her know that we were okay, she was convinced she would never see me alive again. Two years before her death, I was able to send my mother on her own cruise to the beautiful Bahamas, and I'm happy to report there wasn't a terrorist in sight.

I've never thought about this until now, but there were other close calls on that trip. After we arrived in Port Said,

> What happened next was like one of those *I Love Lucy* episodes, except more dangerous than funny.

everyone was eager to put the terrorist scare behind them, and so the plan was to travel by bus to see the pyramids. I decided to remain on the ship for a reason I'll reveal later, and my friend

Helen McVoy, because she had already been to the pyramids, offered to stay onboard with me so that Bruce could go with the others.

What happened next is like one of those *I Love Lucy* episodes, except more dangerous than funny. Helen decided we should use the time to go shopping in this historic Egyptian port city. As we walked from the ship to the street below, a man fell in beside us and announced that he was our guide for the day. We assumed he'd been assigned to be our guide by the tour group, but in fact he had not. We followed him.

Helen told the man we were interested in fine jewelry, so he walked us to a store in town, and for reasons I can't remember, the store was closed to the public but we were ushered inside (a frightening thought). There was much oohing and aahing, and then Helen proceeded to select $17,000 worth of jewelry she thought looked authentically "Egyptian." She handed the shopkeeper her credit card, and though he didn't speak much English and Helen spoke very little Arabic, it soon became pretty clear that the owner would only accept cash. Without missing a beat, Helen said, "No problem. I'll get it from the captain."

The jeweler and our self-proclaimed "guide" took us back to the ship, this time in the storeowner's Mercedes. I guess it was in the car that I began to come to my senses: *two of us being driven in a stranger's car through Port Said by two men whose names we didn't know. Armed with a boatload of jewels and on a mission to get cash from the ship captain.* I prayed I would never leave the safety of the ship again if God would only allow us to make it safely back on board. The men remained in the car while Helen and I walked up the long gangplank of the

> Armed with a boatload of jewels and on a mission to get cash from the ship captain.

Shopping with
Helen McVoy.

ship to find the captain. "I need $17,000 cash," she announced authoritatively, with the conviction of a confident Katharine Hepburn and the smile of a beguiling Julia Roberts. "I'll write you a check." No one *ever* liked telling this woman no. The captain was speechless. He collected his wits sufficient to explain, however, that he didn't keep that kind of cash onboard and advised us that it probably wasn't such a good idea for two American women to be driving around Port Said in the company of two strangers. Well, I was as relieved as Helen was disappointed, but she knew there wasn't any other way to get that jewelry, so she asked *me* to tell the bad news to the men waiting on the street below. I reached the top of the ship's entrance and saw the two eager strangers waiting for us. I suddenly didn't want to be face-to-face with them. My feet froze at the top step. I yelled from the safety of the upper deck, "Sorry, we can't get the money," and then I turned and ran to my room.

> With the terrorist scare fresh in my mind, I ran as fast as I could to get away . . .

Still a little spooked, it was only a few minutes before I thought that danger might be lurking again. As I left my cabin and started down the passageway to Helen's cabin, an Italian crew member yelled very loudly, "Freeze!" and jabbered something in Italian. With the terrorist scare fresh in my mind, I ran as fast as I could to get away—but each time I cleared a cabin, a contraption of heavy metal reminding me of a guillotine came down just behind me. Though I'm still convinced I could have easily been

... my first reaction was At least there were no terrorists on board!

killed had it come down in the split second I was directly underneath it, we later learned it was only a fire drill. The ship crew thought no passengers were on the ship (as everyone had gone to the Pyramids), and the guillotine-like contraptions were fire doors that automatically set off in sequence, one after the other, ultimately closing off each cabin. While I was still in shock, my first reaction was *At least there were no terrorists on board!*

Upon returning from the pyramids and hearing of our adventure, Bruce said if he'd seen me in the backseat of a Mercedes being driven by two strangers through Port Said, he's not sure what he would have done, but he assured me it wouldn't have been pretty. Helen and I sheepishly realized we'd been far too trusting

With Bruce on our eventful cruise aboard the *Stella Solaris.*

and vowed to be changed women when it came to our power shopping urges and staying alone on large ships and running through the cabins during automated fire drills.

Whether it was jetting with Mary Kay Ash to Europe on the *Concorde;* or traveling the countryside on the *Orient Express;* or shopping in Hong Kong, Bangkok, Athens, Jerusalem, Turkey, Venice, Rome, Paris, Monte Carlo, St. Petersburg, or any of many other cities around the world, these Top Ten trips were first-class, dress-up affairs. We were transported in limousines, serenaded by choirs, met by interpreters, entertained like royalty, and treated like queens. You can only imagine, then, the sheer amount of clothing needed by each of us in order to dress properly on these fancy excursions. We never touched our many pieces of luggage after arriving at the departing airport— everything just magically appeared at our destination upon arrival and appeared at our home airport when the trip ended. On our trip to Greece, however, the airline lost our luggage and that of one other couple. On this luxurious Top Ten trip, we were forced to wear the same clothes for four days.

> How low does this V-neck have to sag before we get the airline to do something?

I was okay about it at first, but after wearing the same clothes night and day for ninety-six hours, and once the V-neck sweater I had worn on the flight over began to sag into a low-cut cleavage-revealing look, I'd had enough. "How low does this V-neck have to sag before we get the airline to do something?" I asked. With no luggage in sight, a Mary Kay executive, whose luggage was also lost, was given carte blanche to replace *all* our luggage contents (and his). We started our shopping in the boutiques of the five-star hotel where we were guests and continued from there into the shops around Athens. I never saw the final tally, but having worn

nothing but the clothes on our backs and laundering our underwear in the hotel for four days, we didn't care what would be
charged to the airline—if it fit, we bought it. There was just just
one "little" problem, however: the hotel

I would not trade
one of those trips
with Mary Kay
for anything.

shops didn't sell a full range of men's underwear. Both Bruce and the other husband
without his suitcase were tall, athletic men.
They'd been able to replace some of their
clothes but couldn't find one store in Athens
with underwear large enough to fit them. We trolled the avenues
looking to find an equally tall, athletic man coming out of a store.
Our plan was for our husbands to approach the "target" and ask
him where he bought his underwear. Now, a woman would have
no problem doing that with another woman, but it was terribly
embarrassing for our husbands. Though I hardly remember the
clothes we bought after all these years, the laughter brought on
by mere mention of the "great
underwear hunt" has lasted for
decades.

I would not trade one of
those trips with Mary Kay for
anything. The memories are
priceless, and they seemed to
dissolve the stress of the hard
work that got us there. This was
also the case with my original
offspring Sales Directors. We
worked so hard, but we also
shared the times of our lives
like an extended family.

Once it wasn't a company

My only time on the ski slopes
with Devin in Vail.

trip but a family vacation to the Colorado Mountains that served as a turning point in one particular career. On such trips, the boys usually hit the slopes while I enjoyed après ski. As I routinely did while traveling, I checked in by phone with my key Sales Directors. One of them, Sharon Parris, asked where I was calling from.

"Oh," said Sharon, hardly able to contain the surprise, "I didn't know you were a skier!"

"I'm not," I said. "I came here to think."

That was the day Sharon decided she wanted what I had, and that began her serious work toward the position of National Sales Director. I learned later that she'd hung up the phone that day and told her husband that if this position allowed me to go to such a wonderful place to "think" while spending time with my family, then she wanted that for herself. She wanted that lifestyle for her family, and she got it!

Sometimes it wasn't just the lifestyle that attracted a woman to our business. Joan Chadbourn, a college professor, was introduced to me through a friend who

> I explained that she'd probably be more interested in the 'management' side of becoming a Sales Director . . .

explained that Joan was in the process of relocating with her husband to another city two states over. She asked me if I'd talk to Joan about Mary Kay, and I agreed. The moving van was already in the driveway of her home in Greenville, South Carolina, when I met Joan. Sensing that she didn't feel this would be the right career move for her, I explained that she'd probably be more interested in the "management" side of becoming a Sales Director like me, but in order to do that she would have to start at the beginning and work for at least six months as a Beauty Consultant. Everyone, I explained, begins a Mary Kay business at the same level. She seemed interested, yet she looked at me strangely.

"Doretha, do you know how many degrees, how much education I have?"

"It's okay, Joan," I told her. "We'll accept you anyway."

> Everyone, I explained, begins a Mary Kay business at the same level.

And we did, and she did so well she later became one of the Dingler Area Inner Circle National Sales Directors. She teased me that around the time month-end reports were due, I'd call her to ask what her goals were. She'd tell me what she planned to do the next month. "How about the two days left this month?" I'd ask her, making it very clear there could still be appointments to book, products to sell, and people to meet before that month ended.

I'm proud to know that nearly all of the women I worked with know that I was always committed to their success, even if at times they didn't seem to be. Joan introduced me one year at Seminar by explaining to the audience that my secret was I always urged her to achieve the next challenge and that's the reason she was able to be successful.

Barbara Sunden lived in New Jersey and had done a favor for her sister by hosting a Mary Kay class, after which she decided to give Mary Kay three months. Luckily for us, before she quit, she decided to go to a Mary Kay event and meet Mary Kay Ash in person. Everything changed after that. I watched this stunning,

> They all agreed that number two was not acceptable.

shy, former hairdresser in her early twenties blossom right before my eyes over the course of three decades into a potent force. We still laugh about the Sales Director debut event I attended for Barbara. That's usually a hometown celebration full of friends, family, business associates, and Mary Kay customers. Concerned about the possibility of not having enough attendees at Barbara's debut, however, we went to a nursing home next door and persuaded them to allow some of the residents to come over and be in the audience. To quote the old adage, "It's not where you start, it's where you finish," and Barbara is at the top and continues to set records as the No. 1 NSD.

It was Barbara's leadership in the late 1990s to have "No. 1" ribbons designed and printed and to start a mission for all the NSDs in our Area to unite and make the Dingler Area the number-one Area nationwide! They all agreed that number two was not acceptable. How proud I was to see that mission accomplished: "#1 . . . we did it!" was in print for all of Mary Kay to see at that year's Seminar.

When Barbara Sunden herself was about to be crowned number one nationally for the first of several times, I received a note from her, portions of which I excerpt here:

"So very many times I say to myself, 'What would Doretha do?' when I am searching for the right solution. And I so often quote you when I'm teaching a group of Sales Directors or National Sales Directors. . . . I share so much of what you taught me over the years, and am so grateful for all you have done to mentor, guide, and lead me. I stand in the position today at Mary Kay because of having a Leader like you."

Thank you, Barbara, for those kind words (Barbara has forged a proud legacy for the former Dingler Area by continuing to break company records).

Cheryl Warfield, a beautiful former model and teacher, wanted to progress from Sales Director to National Sales Director. I promised her when she came into my Area that I would do whatever it took to help her achieve this goal. Little did I know the power of those words. Bruce and I traveled to Fort Myers, Florida, and were staying in a hotel on the beach to attend a meeting that evening

In Pink

with Consultants and Directors that would finalize Cheryl's requirements for the NSD qualification period. Suddenly, we began to hear warnings: *Hurricane! Hurricane! Heading toward Fort Myers. . . . Evacuate immediately! Abandon the coast and seek shelter inland!* Everyone was frantic as most residents and visitors on Fort Myers Beach hurriedly

> Nothing, not even a hurricane or an evacuation, was going to stop us.

left. But Cheryl and her husband, Rob, a banker, said, "Please don't leave. We know a safe haven in the bank, underground, if we need to seek shelter." So we stayed and rode out the storm. Long story short, the harrowing ordeal ended with the most damaging of the winds turning away just before hitting land, but from that experience Cheryl and I cemented a bond that will always remain. She was committed to her goal, and I was committed to helping her achieve it. Nothing, not even a hurricane or an evacuation, was going to stop us. Most of her Consultants and Directors came that evening, and everything was completed for her to qualify to go into National Sales Director qualification. Today, she is a very successful Inner Circle National Sales Director from the former Dingler Area!

When Anita Tripp-Brewton came into my area, she was among the youngest Sales Directors I'd ever coached, and she already

> There's not a book big enough for me to recognize all the women who have graced my Mary Kay experience.

knew what her goals were. Most of Anita's training and mentoring came from the late Future National Sales Director, Judy Baker, who tragically lost her life to amyotrophic lateral sclerosis (ALS), also known as Lou Gehrig's diease. Judy was a great friend and a great Director. When I met Anita she was focused on two goals: to be a successful NSD and to have a happy family life. She was a hard worker, and I truly enjoyed watching

108

her reach those goals during the short time I worked with her before my retirement.

There's not a book big enough for me to recognize all the women who have graced my Mary Kay experience. Every day of my life, I think of this wonderful journey with these amazing women. I really do hope they know I will always be there cheering them on—and not just the ones in the winner's circle, but all those women who kept persevering despite life's twists and turns and who continue to teach the principles we value so highly. This is a legacy we all owe to Mary Kay Ash. Better than any highest check amount, she would be truly proudest of the relationships and the bonds that have been borne out of this life-changing experience.

As each year passes, and new goals are achieved, new records broken, I continue to feel a great sense of pride in what the women I mentored achieved and how they will pass it forward. In addition to Joan, Sharon, Barbara, Nan, Anita, and Cheryl,

> . . . I continue to feel a great sense of pride in what the women I mentored achieved . . .

I have utmost respect for the women they've brought into leadership. At the time of my retirement, the other National Sales Directors in the Dingler Area included Heather Armstrong, Gloria Castano, Pam Gruber, Gloryanne Koester, Gerri Nicholson, Sonia Paez, Rita Potter, Patricia Rodriquez-Turker, Robin Rowland, Glinda McGuire, Pam Shaw, Isabel Venegas, and Betty Elliott-Kichler. The list has grown since then as these women in turn have opened doors for more women, and I couldn't begin to count the tens of thousands of Consultants and Directors the former Dingler Area National Sales Directors have now recruited, encouraged, developed, and groomed to be the future leaders of this amazing company.

As this cycle continues and what was the former Dingler

National Area continues to grow, many of the Beauty Consultants, Sales Directors, and National Sales Directors will not have me in their daily lives but perhaps know that I once was the matriarch of their Mary Kay family tree. The quote that opened this chapter bears repeating. It happens to be one Mary Kay Ash loved so much she had it duplicated on little angel magnets she kept in her desk drawer to give to her guests:

> *"We are each of us angels with only one wing; we can only fly by embracing one another."*

NATIONAL
News Notes

Doretha Dingler does it again!
Records are made to be broken.

Independent Executive National Sales Director Doretha Dingler has broken the NSD monthly commission record for a second time. She earned an incredible $104,000 in the month of September! That's the highest monthly commission in Company history and it beats her own record of $97,000 that she set last year.

NATIONAL
News Notes

NSD INNER CIRCLE RECOGNITION

ON-TARGET INNER CIRCLE

On-Target for $1,000,000
Doretha Dingler

For commission totaling one million in one year

Excerpts from National News Notes

Some of our most
memorable trips . . .

Turkey

Paris

The Orient Express

Seeing Europe (quickly)
by bullet train

Welcome to Bangkok,
Thailand!

9

The Quickest Way to a Man's Heart

"Take care of your wife and she'll make you a rich man."
—MARY KAY ASH

I know a lot of you may look at the subject of this chapter as obsolete, a relic of the 1960s that doesn't apply to modern families in which both spouses work and each fully expects to share responsibility for domestic duties such as housekeeping and child care. My first response is that, even in the United States, the extent to which women have been "liberated" from our traditional roles varies widely from region to region and among various ethnic cultures. Even within the most sophisticated, cosmopolitan cities such as New York, there are neighborhoods made up almost entirely of a specific ethnicity where women's roles are as "traditional" as they were when I was speaking to husbands in South Carolina in the 1960s, if not more so.

I also want to point out that Mary Kay is now a truly global company expanding into many developing countries and, although the

> ... Mary Kay is now a truly global company expanding into many developing countries ...

Mary Kay opportunity may be a godsend in a country with few traditional jobs available, many women must still manage strict cultural and religious expectations as to their role in the family before they can begin to build a successful Mary Kay business. For these women, many of whom I hope will be reading this book, being able to win their husband's support is not just helpful, it is downright essential.

> . . . being able to win their husband's support is not just helpful, it is down right essential.

Finally, I would mention the fact that today's family is not as nuclear as it used to be and that one will often find elderly parents, disabled or unemployed siblings, adult children who have returned to the nest because they are un- or underemployed in today's tough job market ("Baby Boomerangs," I believe they're called), and any number of unique configurations wherein people are cohabitating as an economic necessity under the broad umbrella of "family." Right or wrong, it is often the wife/mother in this scenario who becomes the primary caregiver and who therefore must obtain the support of more than the husband to be able to leave the house to attend a sales meeting or hold a class. People quickly become accustomed to being cared for by others, and the same techniques we used with our husbands to "help us help them" back in the good old days are still every bit as relevant to winning the support of anyone who will have to do without us for a few hours now and then in order for everyone to benefit from the Mary Kay opportunity.

> So, for those of you who still have husbands to manage, this chapter is definitely for you

So, for those of you who still have husbands to manage, this chapter is definitely for you. For those of you with other "support-challenged" family members living in your household, simply substitute that person's title (e.g., Mom) for "husband," and you should be good to go. And finally, for you modern women out there living independent, liberated lives with no extended family to support or care for, perhaps you can appreciate what you've missed while taking a few notes for later. You know, just in case.

Most people know how to finish the old saying, "The quickest way to a man's heart is . . ."—through his stomach, right? Well, that's partially true, but there's also another way, and it's something Mary Kay Ash liked to remind our husbands. She thought, and I wholeheartedly agree, that an equally quick way to a man's heart would be through his bank account or, to be more precise, through putting Mary Kay–earned funds *into* his bank account!

> Bruce fully embraced the potential of Mary Kay the day I used one of my checks to buy him a . . . sports car . . .

I was lucky to have benefited from both of these tactics in building my business. From the very beginning, we focused on the family unit while simultaneously helping husbands of our Mary Kay Unit to quickly grasp what was possible if they lent their support to their wife's fledgling new business. In my case, I know that Bruce fully embraced the potential of Mary Kay the day I used one of my checks to buy him a particular sports car he'd had his eye on. By investing in his passion, I secured his commitment to my business and demonstrated

> In the 1960s wives were the supporters of their husband's careers and not vice versa.

unequivocally that this would be a mutually beneficial partnership.

The fascinating thing about the era when I was growing my business is that men—husbands specifically—could be Mary Kay's best friend or its most ardent critic. It all depended on their experience. I've already talked about how in the 1960s wives were the supporters of their husband's careers and not vice versa. When it came to the husbands supporting their wives' careers, that was totally new ground. I was extremely lucky to learn quickly what it was going to take to get the men in our lives to understand our Mary Kay business. It was going to take food.

To be more precise, it was going to take food, mixed with a little friendly competition. We wanted to be sure they understood how this Mary Kay thing worked. The lady of the house would still be their helpmate, but with a little cooperation she could potentially help the family budget as well. We did that on my team by hosting social events to which husbands were invited. We always included three things at those events: food, prizes, and recognition.

At our socials—dubbed covered-dish dinners—the husband would enjoy the meal we served along with the company of other husbands in the Unit. We presented the recognition awards after dinner—"Betty had her highest-class earnings" or "Veronica introduced three potential new team members to this business"—and that's when the husbands would really sit up and take notice.

> We were helping to show the men of our generation that women could do more.

More than one husband new to the social would invariably come up to me after the meeting to confide, "Next time *my* wife will be up there getting a prize or winning a contest." Now that *he* believed and supported the fact that she could do this, most often she did.

I truly believed, and still do today, that this kind of friendly competition became a wonderful vehicle for helping women come into their own. We were helping to show the men of our generation that women could do more. It was usually the case that once they understood it wasn't going to disrupt or disturb the family unit, they were fine. There would be ample family time and time to raise the children, not to mention that the household would still run. I remain very proud that Mary Kay wanted us to achieve our success without sacrificing our families. She believed it wasn't much fun to be successful if you had no one to share that success with. Certainly times have changed so that today the majority of women do work and balance is more important than ever, but there is a timeless element to this message that never changes.

> She believed it wasn't much fun to be successful if you had no one to share that success with.

Mary Kay Ash personally applauded our efforts, as she voiced on so many occasions when she reiterated that her intention was *never* for this business to come between a woman and her family life, and especially her married life. Fact is, the kind of success we were experiencing was a heady thing, and that's why emphasizing the importance of family values in Mary Kay's success equation started from the very beginning and continues today.

We also had some additional practical measures that helped reassure the husbands. This was long before cell phones or text messaging, so we encouraged Beauty Consultants to call home once they arrived at an evening meeting, to call again when they were on the way home, and to call in between those times if they saw they were going to be home later than planned. When Bruce or I visited with husbands in our Unit, we'd explain why they needed to allow their wives the time to focus on these meetings, classes, and events and to be supportive when they were held in the evening. We always took pains to explain why it occasionally needed to be evenings: so that other women could attend while their husbands were home with the children.

In my own family, we tried to have time that didn't involve

Mary Kay. I'll be the first to admit there is always the temptation to weave this kind of work into every single thing you do every day—to breathe, eat, and sleep it 24/7. Driven as I was, even I got pretty good at unplugging the phone when it was family time. Bruce and I had long since decided this would be a good routine to follow. We liked spending good, quality time with Devin—we didn't want him to be raised by anyone but us. When we needed to travel during the years before he was in school, we all traveled together. I still have a sample of Bruce and Devin's extensive collection of library cards—assembled as they accompanied me on my Mary Kay journey in the early days of my career. They needed things to do in towns where I was hosting a guest

Taking time out to host a Halloween party for Devin.

event or teaching a class, and joining the local library was ideal for both. Today they're still inveterate readers.

I also need to be candid and admit I never had a natural desire to be a "domestic goddess." Oh, I could cook (sort of) but didn't really love it, nor did I learn at a young age since I was at my dad's business anytime I could get there. When Devin was little, I was Cub Scout den mother, wife of a busy professional, and prided myself on throwing parties for holidays and birthdays. We loved our family vacations with Devin, and the Mary Kay checks were just tremendous at affording us this luxury. One of the nicest compliments Mary Kay ever paid me was when she told me I was

> I was Cub Scout den mother, wife of a busy professional, and prided myself on throwing parties for holidays and birthdays.

a good role model and included a brief capsule of my I Story in one of the earliest recruiting brochures. I was portrayed as the

> I also need to be candid and admit I never had a natural desire to be a 'domestic goddess.'

happy homemaker, which indeed I was. That description stuck, even as I was being honored onstage as a pink Cadillac earner or when I became a National Sales Director in 1974 presiding over thousands of Directors and Consultants.

It really did seem like the harder I worked, the luckier I got—as that old saying goes. I wrote in an earlier chapter about taking care of yourself and how so many women never learned to do that as they were primarily focused on taking care of others. In the years after I became a National Sales Director, sometimes it took not only those long soaks in the tub but also massages to get me through the stress of the work. I still advise women to choose something that helps them be their best while working toward a big goal. That something might be anything from massage therapy to baking a cherry pie from scratch or running a mile at dawn—whatever works. Learning to deal with the stresses of your work is key in continuing to handle all the plate spinning we women are called upon to do.

We knew the importance of having our husbands solidly behind us! The sports car I was able to buy for Bruce with one of my checks continued to keep his attention. Another sales director purchased a golf membership for her husband. Mary Kay liked this message and our family-oriented

Devin and Bruce, with the car I bought for him with just one Mary Kay check.

team. She liked to see women getting caught up in achieving their goals while working equally hard at maintaining their families. She always knew we needed to do more teaching in this area so that

women could be better prepared for moving up the career ladder while keeping their priorities in balance. One year, she asked me to travel with renowned motivational speaker Zig Ziglar to lecture on family values and success. I read recently that Zig says it was in teaching those early lectures for the Mary Kay audiences

On "tour" with Zig Ziglar.

that he changed his life's philosophy. After being discovered by Mary Kay audiences, he authored nine best sellers and has been called an authority on the science of human potential. His organization spans the globe today, and I was honored to have been one of those who went on the road with Zig to teach Mary Kay's message. Mary Kay Ash is regularly listed among the handful of people who exerted the most influence on Zig's life.

Mary Kay also asked me—and eventually Bruce—to teach a husband's class at Seminar. New Beauty Consultants and Sales Directors were encouraged to have their husbands travel with them to Dallas not only to get the big picture of the company, but also to meet and get to know other husbands who were experiencing this new phenomenon or whose wives were enjoying success. Mary Kay Ash and her son Richard Rogers recognized early the importance of helping the men understand, and they sponsored these spouse classes for the very reasons I organized covered-dish suppers.

The first year I taught the husband's class at Seminar, I wanted it attended by husbands only—I requested that none of the male executives from the corporation (or my husband) should attend. I asked two of my most vivacious Sales Directors to host the class with me, and they were so wonderful at painting the picture of their success while emphasizing the family values they both held in high regard. We spoke sincerely of the importance of our own families and husbands. We tried to paint a picture of what the women they loved needed from them in order to do well with a Mary Kay business. We served the men refreshments. It was a big hit!

> We tried to paint a picture of what the women they loved needed from [their husbands] in order to do well with a Mary Kay business

I'll never forget when Bruce addressed the husbands at Seminar at the beginning of my Directorship in the late 1960s. His words were heartfelt and genuine. He'd always told me to "Do what you need to do, and I'll be behind you," but hearing him share that day gave me a new realization of just how important it was that he understood the message that so many husbands needed to hear. Here is one small excerpt from that speech that I still find particularly poignant:

> *"It dawned on me one day that I wasn't excited or enthusiastic about what I was doing, where I was going, or where I wanted to go in my own profession. It occurred to me that it was time that I made a change—to get into a business I really enjoyed. And here's the beautiful part. I was like many people who would make such a decision in their lives if they could see where they could get the capital to sustain them while they were getting established. That's where Mary Kay came in. The income from my wife's Mary Kay directorship provided our family that capital."*

As with so much about our life, Mary Kay was right again. Hearing my own husband's speech that day reinforced for me that I'd made a good decision. Hearing him speak about what a difference my income had made in his work life and job satisfaction made me even prouder.

Many years later, we were with one of the couples we'd been friends with since the wife and I attended that first Mary Kay wig party in Greenville, Texas. As dinner table talk turned to my Mary Kay success, the husband gently chided his wife, asking her why she didn't stay with the Mary Kay business and find the success I'd found. "I might have," she said unapologetically, "if you hadn't insisted dinner be on the table every night at six p.m."

'I might have . . . if you hadn't insisted dinner be on the table every night at six p.m.'

10

Mary Kay and Me

(Oprah and the Horatio Alger Award)

"It is leaders like you who have made our Company great."

—MARY KAY ASH TELEGRAM TO DORETHA DINGLER,
APRIL 8, 1976

Me and Mary Kay.

ary Kay Ash remains one of those famous and iconic leaders who was everything they say she was and then some. In her business model, she used concepts that many didn't even recognize, and she was using them well before many experts realized how positively such principles could impact a business. She created a company of friends that praises you when you deserve praise, gives you ideas when you need them, and nudges you a little when you need that. In relating my story, it's important you know that I consider it a privilege to have my name in the same sentence as this legend—not to mention the honor I feel to have considered her a friend.

This one woman had such an incredible impact on my life and the lives of countless millions of women throughout the world. The fact that I knew a legend up close and personal was brought home to me several years ago when a busload of women came to my home for a party celebrating their Seminar accomplishments. They, of course, wanted to tour the house. Some of them asked if it was okay if they took photos of themselves in my bathtub. I said okay, and then I stepped into a back room to hold back tears. It's not that my bathtub was anything special—and it wasn't even *pink*. What hit me was the sentiment. You see, there's a much-storied tradition that began when Mary Kay and Mel moved into the beautiful round house Mel designed for her. There was a beautiful boudoir with a pink marble bathtub, and it became a hallowed tradition that was said to bring good luck to all Sales Directors to have their photo taken in the tub. It was such a strong sentiment that a former president of the company made it a practice to have a replica of the round pink bathtub, without the plumbing, displayed in his office at Mary Kay world headquarters when new Sales Directors visited Dallas for their meetings. Lines

Nelta Dellinger posing for the traditional bathtub photo in my home.

and lines of new Sales Directors would stand for hours patiently waiting to climb into the replica of that pink good luck charm and have their photo taken in it—just as they had done at Mary Kay's home. Now here they were *in my bathtub* thinking that same good luck might somehow have been passed along to me. I felt an enormous wave of gratitude to be considered part of Mary Kay's sacred bathtub legacy.

> She loved the fact that it had taken a termination letter to get me moving.

Mary Kay was a woman who liked establishing traditions. She also liked challenges and those who overcame them. She appreciated my small-town Texas country roots. She loved the fact that it had taken a termination letter to get me moving forward in this business, and she encouraged me to relate this story every time I took the stage. She thought it was a classic example of the fact that it doesn't take long to go from the bottom to the top once you have everything in the proper perspective. I am a great poster child for the song most closely associated with the position of National Sales Director—in fact, according to tradition, all the Nationals perform a kick line to it onstage at every Seminar. The song is "It's Not Where You Start, It's Where You Finish."

Mary Kay liked that message because it gave everyone from every background hope. Just because we were housewives and mothers didn't mean we couldn't exercise our talents and develop our unique strengths in business. A stable home, she'd say, provides a wonderful base from which to flourish. And a supportive family, she told us, makes us twice the woman. She

> She appreciated that the roots of my success had spread far outside the confines of Texas.

appreciated that the roots of my success had spread far outside the confines of Texas. She knew many people referred to her company as "Mary Who" and could appreciate how it must have been for those of us in the early days who were out in the heartland quite a distance from the Texas headquarters. She also liked it when we related the challenges we'd overcome. Like that time I took a potential recruit to observe a class and no one showed. Or when I had some of the newest on my team attend a class to learn how to sell, and no one attending the class bought anything. "No one can hold you back in Mary Kay," Mary Kay told us, "except for you." Her business philosophy was that sharing ideas meant your ideas were multiplied.

Mary Kay loved it when husbands understood our company's unique culture. She always enjoyed hearing Bruce relate how different her model was from the corporate structures he was familiar with—some of the most successful companies in the engineering and aviation fields. They talked about what a refreshing change it was that the Mary Kay sales force never has to climb over someone to be successful, that we never have to wait for someone to

> Not many people even realize that when Oprah was inducted into the Horatio Alger Association, it was longtime member Mary Kay Ash who placed that medal around Oprah's neck.

retire so that we can get ahead. As we would come to know first-hand, a Mary Kay business could be relocated or transferred just about anywhere. She never failed to point out that there are "women with skin" everywhere. We talked about how often we met women with great potential, who just couldn't make the leap. It prompted us to create a favorite saying: "Except for me, there go I."

The entire trajectory of our family had been changed by the career opportunity Mary Kay provided. She was proud that Bruce had been able to change careers and go out on his own, thanks to my earnings. So many times in our lives, it was Mary Kay who was in our amen corner and who served as the encourager we needed.

Mine Is Not to Question Why

Mary Kay is a woman whose story is told alongside those of everyone from Henry Ford to Oprah Winfrey to Bill Gates, and yet she could empathize with the everyday happenings in ordinary lives like ours. Not many people even realize that when Oprah was inducted into the Horatio Alger Association, it was longtime member Mary Kay Ash who placed that medal around Oprah's neck.

Mary Kay often emphasized that nothing was more important than reaching out and touching other lives. When Mary Kay met a pediatrician who'd given up her medical practice to be a Sales Director, she cautioned her company publicists to hold the story until the doctor had proven herself—wanting to send a message that it doesn't matter who you are, it's what you do with your career that tells the story and that will have the most impact on others, as does Oprah's story.

Mary Kay and Bruce had a good relationship because she knew he "got it." She honored him beyond words when she asked that he serve as a pallbearer at her husband Mel's funeral. We loved Mel, and especially the fact that he adored Mary Kay. From the day that she and Mel had their first date, he gave her a gift every week for the rest of his life as a way of honoring that special occasion. We were delighted when Mel would refer to himself as the

Bruce with Mary Kay.

"chairman of the chairman of the board." He and Mary Kay had the kind of loving and supportive relationship she cherished and wanted for all of us because she knew how important that was.

Mary Kay had such a down-to-earth, practical side to her business and personal life. She delighted in sharing a piece of pie with Bruce one time in Bangkok. Both had a sweet tooth, and either could've easily finished the entire piece of pie, on their own, and

certainly could have afforded it, but Bruce and Mary Kay agreed to share the pie because the price was too high. She and Bruce laughed about that and the fact that both at the time were reluctantly counting calories.

Much has been said about the strict professional dress code Mary Kay established. Some have taken that to mean she intended we wear business suits around the clock. That's not the case—as all of us who saw her in the garden she loved or traveling internationally can attest. I have a photo of us shopping together in

Shopping in Hong Kong with Mary Kay wearing her Dallas Jeans.

1987 in Hong Kong with her wearing a denim pantsuit festooned with a gold oil derrick and an outline of the state of Texas.

We shared so many wonderful trips together that hardly a day goes by I don't think of something wonderful or wise or witty I learned from Mary Kay Ash. Whether shopping for jewelry in the markets of Europe, where she made sure none of us spent too much of our hard-earned money, or whether by her

> I sometimes had to pinch myself to realize I was experiencing the world with the woman I consider one of the world's most phenomenal leaders.

setting the example, we all summoned up the courage to ride a camel in the desert, I sometimes had to pinch myself to realize I

Bruce's tour of China.

was experiencing the world with the woman I consider one of the world's most phenomenal leaders. Those early trips with Mary Kay and the Top Ten National Sales Directors will always be among the greatest memories of my life. With her inimitable style of making people feel important, she made all of us feel special as she spent time with each of us individually on these trips. She visited each table between courses so she could spend quality time with all of us. She liked that we shared camaraderie and a sisterhood, shopping secrets and business tips. Who does that as well as Mary Kay? Not one person I've ever met.

When we visited Asia and some in the group, including Bruce, were able to get permission to travel into China, Mary Kay was curious enough to encourage them to truly check out what was going on in that vast nation. Before she died, Mary Kay was aware that modern-day China had become the company's largest market outside the United States, that the women of that nation and many others had the utmost respect for her and for her vision to help women everywhere. A company executive who had been

> Mary Kay was aware that modern-day China had become the company's largest market outside the United States.

detained on that trip for security reasons was later instrumental in seeing China's potential a good while before other companies followed suit. He'd been among a handful of American corporate executives who wholeheartedly accepted an invitation from the Chinese government to visit China on a trade mission that led to establishment of Mary Kay operations and eventually a manufacturing facility there.

In later years when she wasn't on a particular trip, Mary Kay loved the stories we brought back. She got a big kick when she heard the story of a Mary Kay trip during which a male company executive couldn't be seated at our posh dinner because he wasn't wearing a tie. She delighted in how we problem solved on that one. Some of us took him around the corner from the restaurant and got him to take off his socks, and then we fashioned a rather spiffy-looking bow tie out of the socks. In short order, we arrived back at the restaurant, where we were then promptly seated.

In 1977 the company planned what was supposed to be an elegant NSD retreat at a remote lodge at Tan-Tar-A, Osage Beach, Missouri, on Lake of the Ozarks. It turned out that to get there we had to fly puddle-jumper planes that also carried chained

Those early trips with Mary Kay and the Top Ten National Sales Directors will always be among the greatest memories of my life.

Mary Kay learning to ride a camel.

Experiencing a new mode of transportation (with a little help from Bruce).

prisoners being transported to a jail nearby. The lodge was so massive that we had to have golf carts transport us in our high-heeled,

It turned out that to get there we had to fly puddle-jumper planes that also carried chained prisoners

bejeweled, dressy-casual finery from our cabins on the property to the meeting room.

The first morning we convened as a group, Mary Kay was listening to the opening remarks when all of a sudden her shoulders started shaking (like you do in church when you're trying to be reverent and something funny just takes over your entire being) as she tried to conceal uncontrollable laughter. Soon enough, the speaker stopped and all eyes in the room were trained on her. Mary Kay's expressive eyes were filled with laughter-induced tears by the time she explained herself. Here she was trying to give her leaders the ultimate in luxury at our first National Sales Directors retreat, when what we got was a men's hunting lodge in the rough and all that implied. She later explained that she lost it when she looked up to where there should be chandeliers and saw instead exposed pipes and beams in the cavernous ceiling after we'd been flown in on planes carrying prisoners and transported in all our finery via rustic golf carts. All of this had just suddenly seemed hysterically funny to her. I often wonder if that's when the decision was made to make sure future National Sales Director trips were first class in every way: like flying on the *Concorde,* being picked up in Rolls Royces in world capitals, and staying in five-star hotels with apartment-size suites etc., etc.

... she lost it when she looked up to where there should be chandeliers and saw instead exposed pipes and beams in the cavernous ceiling ...

One time when Mary Kay was ailing, she asked if I'd step in for her to make a speech in Cincinnati. A marching band that had been planned for her met me at the airport, and I saw up close the kind of adoration women everywhere reserve for Mary Kay.

Another time, I was onstage with her at an event when security had to intervene because the crowd was pushing too close to the stage and to Mary Kay herself. After her talk, we were escorted by security through the hotel kitchen. We'd almost made a clean break for her waiting motorcade, when suddenly Mary Kay spied some of the women who hadn't been able get into the ballroom for her appearance. They'd gathered in a side hallway hoping to at least catch a glimpse of the legend. Much to security's chagrin and heedless of crowd control, Mary Kay promptly made her way to greet and mingle with these women. She told us later that it was the least she could do since they'd been unable to get into the packed ballroom by order of the fire marshal.

> Much to security's chagrin and heedless of crowd control, Mary Kay promptly made her way to greet and mingle with these women.

With Mary Kay at the St. Louis Cardinal's game.

When Mary Kay was asked to throw out the first pitch at a St. Louis Cardinals baseball game in Missouri, I was among the Sales Directors invited to attend that event with her. Way back then, no one knew that a fund-raising athletic event like this would be a precursor to the "Pink at the Park" benefit ballgames in various sports that today benefit Mary Kay's Foundation and others.

Speaking of her foundation, one of my proudest moments came in 1996, the year the Mary Kay Ash Foundation came to be. Mary Kay invited me to serve on the foundation's Advisory Coun-

With Mary Kay while attending a Mary Kay Foundation meeting held in her home.

cil. Meeting at her home for one of our first gatherings was a remarkably poignant day because earlier that same year Mary Kay Ash had suffered a stroke that robbed her of her incredible voice. Few of us had seen her since the stroke. That day as we gathered around her, it was the first time she wasn't able to converse with us. There were awkward moments at first, but Mary Kay communicated to us with her expressive eyes and gestures. We sensed immediately that she needed us, her National Sales Directors, to take up the conversation in her place. And so we did, and the photos from that day are priceless reminders. She always told us she and her son, Richard, had created the position of National Sales Director to be an extension of herself. That June day in 1996 was the first day many of us realized

> Meeting at her home for one of our first gatherings was a remarkably poignant day . . .

that the inevitable day, that time, had now come. It was time for us to be her voice. As sobering and somber a realization as it was, all of us knew she had prepared us well. We let her know we were confident that all our sister National Sales Directors would be up to the challenge.

Mary Kay Ash would never return to the office, to the company, or to the day-to-day activity she had loved for so many years.

> She wanted to convey to everyone that she, indeed, was passing the baton to her first generation of leaders.

She made a valiant effort that same summer to attend Seminar, and bravely wore the gorgeous white evening gown that had been designed for her before the stroke. At each of the next five Seminars, she stood onstage (with assistance) as tens of thousands of women poured out their heart, their applause, and their tears to her. For each of her appearances, Mary Kay asked that her National Sales Directors be gathered beside and around her onstage. She wanted to convey to everyone that she, indeed, was passing the baton to her first generation of leaders. I will never forget the message she prepared, that she asked be read by a National Sales Director. She thanked us for blessing her life. Unable to speak, she waved and touched her heart at the huge outpouring of love, the response from all these women for whom she had played such a momentous role. At one of the meetings, miraculously she was somehow able to haltingly utter a few words. There was a silenced hush in the arena. It was the last time anyone was to hear that voice; the last time we were to hear from that champion of womankind who had poured so much into our lives.

Mary Kay spoke clearly enough that everyone understood: "You can do it."

Those same four words her own mother had spoken to her as a child—when Mary Kay was afraid or feeling less than able to accomplish something. Her mother would gently persuade her, *You can do it.* And on this momentous day, every one in that huge convention center and beyond believed we could indeed.

11

Interstitial Cystitis— Medical Challenge Defied

"Life is a voyage in which we choose neither vessel nor weather, but much can be done in management of the sails and the guidance of the helm."
—AUTHOR UNKNOWN

According to the Interstitial Cystitis Association (ICA), Interstitial cystitis (IC) is a chronic painful condition of the bladder. Symptoms are similar to a bladder infection but unresponsive to antibiotics. About four million Americans suffer from IC. It can be a debilitating condition that negatively impacts nearly every aspect of a person's life. Because of the complexity of the disease and lack of clear understanding, it may take up to five years to obtain a diagnosis. In severe cases, IC patients suffer from unrelenting pain that necessitates trips to the bathroom for relief as often as every ten to fifteen minutes—both during the day and at night. Some people with IC have symptoms that prevent them from leaving their home or even riding in a car, greatly limiting or preventing their ability to work, travel, or participate in leisure activities. More research is needed to understand all aspects of IC, including variations in treatments. A number of promising clinical trials testing potentially new IC treatments are underway (Interstitial Cystitis Association: www.ichelp.org).

And according to the Mayo Clinic, IC can have a long-lasting, adverse effect on quality of life. There is no known cause, no reliable treatment, and no cure. Some medications and therapies offer some relief (www.mayoclinic.com/health/interstitial-cystitis/ DS00497).

> I believe it was turning these negatives into positives that helped mold me into who I am today.

I have IC and am fortunate to have been under the care of a doctor who encouraged me not to leave this significant chapter of my life out of this book.

When I was five years old, I was run over by a car driven by a thirteen-year-old kid who'd taken his mother's vehicle. At the hospital that day, I overheard the doctors telling my parents that if it weren't for the miracle that this happened on a street where the soil was very sandy (even though it happened within the city limits of Athens, all streets were not paved, luckily for me), I might not have survived. The weight of the car buried me in the sand, saving me from certain death, but it damaged my internal organs to an extent that I didn't really comprehend until much later in my life. Afterward, it was as if this horrible accident never happened. It was rarely discussed in family conversation. My siblings weren't even born yet, and my mother said it was too painful to talk about.

I actually spoke with the person who ran over me years later during a visit in 1989 to Athens for a funeral, and he told me the accident had bothered him every day of his life. He seemed relieved to see me looking so well. And for me, after so many years to finally have the accident acknowledged, especially by this person, was, in a weird way, some comfort.

One of the lifelong consequences of the injuries sustained in that accident was that I was left with a small bladder. I figured it was just another obstacle I could overcome, and I handled it the same way my family had as I was growing up: I didn't talk about it.

Building the Dingler National Area while managing this medical condition that went undiagnosed and undertreated for years is hard for me to comprehend. In 1974, three months into my NSD position, I had what I thought was a bladder infection and was put on antibiotics, but the symptoms of the infection continued, even after taking a full course of the antibiotics, and tissue cultures showed no infection. Thus began a classic diagnosis of IC, but in 1974 doctors didn't know much about this condition. I was told to see a psy-

> Building the Dingler National Area while managing this medical condition that went undiagnosed and undertreated for years is hard for me to comprehend.

chiatrist because, frankly, they simply didn't know how to treat me. Actually it was not until the 1980s that IC began gaining attention in the medical profession, but doctors still had no reliable treatment available to them. I consider myself fortunate that while living in Dallas during the 1980s, I was referred to Dr. Arthur

With Dr. Arthur Shannon and his wife, Leila

Shannon, a highly respected urologist, whose treatment helped me get through some difficult times.

In my case, I have a notion that my childhood trauma was a precursor to my diagnosis, but that's never been medically confirmed. Whatever the cause, I've had to figure out on my own the boundaries I had to set in my life in order to live, work, and function as normally as possible with IC. Knowing the things I could and couldn't do was something I had to learn by trial and error. Bruce and I were told it would be wise for me not to have any more children—that it could compromise my already weakened bladder. Yet despite years of frustration, I believe it was turning these negatives into positives that helped mold me into who I am today.

It's only been in recent years that I was even aware that support groups for IC had been established. My hope is that there will be more effective medications available in the near future to manage IC more successfully and to prevent drastic situations such as the suicide of someone in the support group I later joined.

I believe that having a supportive family and the can-do spirit of the Mary Kay world around me has made my management of IC less stressful. Because it's considered a very serious condition, for me to accomplish what I did *despite this condition* has been one of my life's greatest challenges. It's awkward to have a conversation about IC with almost anyone other than your doctor and close family.

Out to dinner and feeling great with Dr. Casey Caldwell and his wife, Robin.

"You are a survivor if I've ever seen one," said Dr. Casey Caldwell of the Mayo Clinic in Rochester, Minnesota, where I've gone for treatment with this specialist in internal medicine for more than twenty-five years. "I so admire the way you've always refused to let this condition define you."

> It's awkward to have a conversation about IC with almost anyone other than your doctor and close family.

Dr. Caldwell was one of the few people I could have my pity parties with, as he seemed to always grasp the significance of my doing what I did when flare-ups occurred, and most of all never knowing when or where I would have one. Once when I was at a particularly low point, he confided, "I know people with acne or a migraine who complain more than you, and whose conditions are the reason they haven't attained their goals." Unaccustomed as I am to being so open about this, I'm glad he encouraged me to talk about it. For one thing, it explains some of the quirky things I did. It was a feeling of constantly being brought to my knees while in the midst of following what would for most be a normal routine. It was a lifestyle that wouldn't seem to fit in with the work I needed to do, but I was determined to do it anyway. I once chewed off the entire top of a pencil eraser on a California freeway we couldn't exit as a way to distract myself from the pain I was experiencing. For all those times people thought I was being extra-inquisitive—about the specifications of the bus that was taking us to the pyramids of Egypt, or which plane we were flying into Vail, or even how far the ladies room was from the meeting room—I had good reason. For everyone who might have

> It was a lifestyle that wouldn't seem to fit in with the work I needed to do, but I was determined to do it anyway.

wondered why I chose to remain back at the hotel for a spa day instead of taking an excursion to some exotic locale, this was my way of normalizing what was not a normal life at all. As for the limousine drivers in Italy—like the one who had to hastily exit to the side of a remote mountainside road— I'm sure they thought I was just one more eccentric American. When I had to be persist-

With our limo driver in Italy.

ent about which pew we needed to be seated on in the church sanctuary, I just couldn't be concerned with what others thought. Painful, humiliating, and embarrassing as it was, there was something inside me that kept telling me nothing was going to keep me from going on with my life, even as these rude and inconvenient interruptions continued.

Of course, those few who did know about it understood I had to live a different way. The experts say IC alters your life 100 percent. However, I can honestly say I have never considered quitting at anything. When I hear of people whose dreams were smashed because of chronic conditions, it makes me all the more convinced that I chose the right course: to keep on keeping on.

> I chose the right course: to keep on keeping on.

My feeling today is that being able to change lives, work with such wonderful women, and get to know Mary Kay Ash more than made up for my challenges. As long as IC can somehow be managed, my every intention has always been to not just manage it, but to control it and not ever allow it to control me.

My entire life, when people have told me things were impossible, I've had this attitude of "Find a way, or make a way." Dr. Caldwell, who knows about that Mary Kay termination letter I received, tells me the way I reacted (going from termination to the top) was a good indication of how I would behave all those times when things got tough with my health. I also think it might have provided me the strength to help others keep on going when they faced challenges.

I once read the story of how a lobster grows and thought that sounded a lot like me. You may know that the shell is so hard that a lobster must learn to shed it at regular intervals. But when it sheds that shell, the lobster is left extremely vulnerable. Basically the lobster has to risk its own life to grow.

Years ago, I read about the lobster in a book about the crisis of middle age. I think it applies to the way I look at life. It's about how we endure the passage of time and the limits of our mortality. The

> There are times in all our lives when only we can know it is time to take a risk.

way we do that is to know we are growing and changing and that we are, indeed, becoming more. We should all, I firmly believe, have a sense of those times in our life when that "lobster shell" is getting too tight. We should not waste a minute shedding it, lest we feel stifled or even smothered in our shell. There are times in all our lives when only we can know it is time to take a risk.

How fortunate I feel that, because of Mary Kay, I've been able to take all the risks I needed in order to grow and to thrive. To run not walk. To decide I wanted this career, and to work, alter situations, and play toward it every day. We have been granted the power to choose exactly where we want to go in life. To decide where and how we want to spend all 86,400 seconds of every day. Despite the obstacles, I never wasted a second, and for that I'm extremely proud.

"Most people live and die with their music still unplayed. They never dare to try." Fortunately, that favorite saying of Mary Kay Ash does not describe my life. And for me, at the end of the day, that is what I am most thankful for.

12

The Most Important Pages in My Scrapbook

"Mary Kay asked that we take our families along on this journey. She knew that if we mold ourselves into positive, inspiring role models for our families, they would have a head start on living their own journey successfully."

—MARY KAY INC. TRIBUTE WEBSITE,
DORETHA DINGLER QUOTE

It's been nine years since I added "Emeritus" to my title. The word *emeritus* is Latin for one who is retired but retains the former title. People have asked me why I didn't write this book any sooner—you know: strike while the iron is hot—especially when I was so fortunate to finish my career at the very top of the sales force. Some have reasoned that a lot more people would've known me. A lot more people would perhaps have been compelled to read my story. More people might buy my book.

As an entrepreneur, I agree with that line of reasoning. However, as the person who lived my life, I believe the story is so much more heartfelt, more vivid today since I've had more time to reflect. Much like my own life, the evolution of this story is richer for having had this time to better understand it. I was married eight years before Devin was born; I was retired eight years before starting to give birth to my memoir.

My favorite picture of Brittany, age three.

Actually, it was in the months before Bruce and I celebrated our golden wedding anniversary that it occurred to me that Brittany, the only child of our only child, didn't really know us. I mean, she knew us and we've always been extremely close, but since we'd already lived a full life by the time she was born, she knew us as . . . *ahem* . . . older people. I could hear in the kinds of questions she asked us that she wanted to know more about so many things in our lives. As Bruce and I put together the scrapbooks for our golden anniversary celebration with the help of my assistant of more than twenty years, Paula Funderburk, I finally felt compelled. It seemed as if this was the right time to tell my story. In fact, I was more than compelled. I felt an overwhelming desire

> I felt an overwhelming desire to reflect back over this amazing journey.

to reflect back over this amazing journey after I realized how much Brittany loved the scrapbook of her own life we did for her when she was about to graduate high school. Her parents told us how they found her paging through it, asking questions about this detail and that. There were hints she was curious to know more about her family. She loved hearing the fact that her grandfather was a successful athlete, since she is a fine athlete herself and is now a freshman member of her college's varsity volleyball team. When we'd mention that we'd traveled to someplace she was studying in world history class, she was curious. "You've been there, Dee Dee!" she'd exclaim. "Tell me what it was like."

Bruce with Turner Gauntt receiving the Outstanding Back and Lineman of the year awards.

So it became front burner urgent for me to capture the memories flooding my mind as we began putting the golden anniversary scrapbooks and photo albums together. It seemed like this would be the perfect time to paint the full picture for Brittany, just as I had done all those years for the thousands of women I mentored in Mary Kay.

One day in a meeting with our family estate planner, the conversation about my business led to my explaining to her in more

Paula (my assistant of more than 20 years) with husband, John.

detail what it was that I had done in my career. This successful and very smart professional made a statement that went to the heart of the story when she observed that my success had unfolded during one of the most important eras for women. I read the same kind of observation in a *Newsweek* piece published in March 2010. "There will be many a 50-year anniversary to reflect/mark the significant events of the 1960s. . . . What happened in that remarkable era still resonates today."

Maybe that's one of the reasons I devoted so much space in this book to talking about "how it was in my day." It seems to me that women of younger generations need to have an appreciation for what has preceded the freedoms and the privileges that were unheard of when I was a young girl. I believe that the more positive examples, the more personal stories of the way we were, the better it is for all of us. I'm very proud of the pioneer position that I occupied at the top of the sales force in one of our nation's most beloved companies. I truly believe my experiences hold lessons not just for my granddaughter but for future generations as well.

> I truly believe my experiences hold lessons not just for my granddaughter but for future generations as well.

Today as I hear our talented granddaughter discuss with ease everything from the Nineteenth Amendment to the latest best seller to her finest volleyball maneuver, I am struck even more by the desire to shower her with a genealogy laced with perspective from my own generation.

It seems like only yesterday when Devin would bring Brittany to our house in the wee hours of the morning as he and her mom were on their way to their jobs. We'd let Brittany sleep a couple extra hours, then enjoy breakfast with her before Bruce carted her off to school for the day. Neither one of us would trade that experience for anything on earth. And it has made us extra appreciative of the career that allowed us to relocate so our granddaughter could grow up with us around. Rather than material things, it is these extra opportunities Mary Kay afforded us that we appreciate the most. As they say, "Anyone can make a living." We were able to make such a life.

Brittany in her favorite heart shirt.

Brittany tells us how proud she was to be picked up from school in my pink Cadillac. All the elementary students would gather in a huge glassed-in lobby for afternoon carpool pickup, and because of all the commotion caused when the other children saw a pink Cadillac pulling into the drive through, Brittany knew it was her favorite time of the day—time for her to bound outside, jump into the front seat with her Papa (and me in the backseat), and give us each a big hug. She loved dining with us a couple times a week at a favorite restaurant in Dallas's Preston Center, and she was always amused when a Mary Kay person would recognize me and come over to our table. I was just Dee Dee to Brittany, but she observed the respect I would show to others, even when I was attempting to enjoy a piece of pecan pie. In fact, I was practicing one of Mary Kay's greatest teachings: "MMFI—Make Me Feel Important," a concept that is now taught in college classrooms.

Trying to pose for a picture with two-year-old Brittany.

In addition to noticing how we treated people, Brittany loves the memory of the 1950s rock-and-roll music Bruce and I played as we drove her all over Dallas, my fingers snapping time to the music. She still laughs when she recalls how "perky" I would get whenever an Elvis song came on the radio. She also vividly recalls that day she discovered something she'd never known about me. As she says, "I was upstairs with the TV blaring when all of a sudden I heard this amazing music coming from downstairs. I thought maybe Dee Dee had put a new tape on. I liked it and wanted to hear it better, so I went bounding down the stairs. There's my Dee

Dee at the piano, bouncing to the up-tempo jazzy piece she was playing on the piano!"

One of my favorite recent memories is when Brittany was studying advanced economics her junior year of high school. The textbook chapter, "Leading Entrepreneurs," featured Mary Kay Ash. "I realized what it was that my Dee Dee had done. I knew she was one of the first to help Mary Kay be a frontrunner in the business world," she says today.

Brittany in her Highland Park Presbyterian Day School uniform.

"Growing up, I wasn't exactly sure what my Dee Dee did, but I always thought she was the boss of lots of people (she didn't realize there are no bosses in Mary Kay); she had so many beautiful things that were pink, and she got huge boxes of free makeup all the time—and she let me have as much of it as I wanted."

With Brittany on Grandparents' Day at The Bement School.

Brittany is now in college, and I'm thrilled to report that she is an honor student with so much potential. Brittany tells me she learned about the need to set goals from growing up in the Mary Kay world. We have thoroughly enjoyed watching her grow up and become the person any grandparent would be proud of—how lucky we are!

As I collected my thoughts for our scrapbook material, it occurred to me that in addition to Brittany being the right age to hear all I had to say, there might be others who'd benefit, others who might also learn something from my story. It was a feeling I'd experienced before. If you've read the book thus far, you know that was the same reaction I'd had way back in 1969 when Mary Kay first asked me to share some of my success secrets with my sister Sales Directors. As fearful as I was of actually speaking to them, once it was over I had the same feeling. *Maybe,* I thought at that time, *if Mary Kay thinks I have something to say, maybe I do.* And so this memoir took on a purpose larger than its original intent. I came to understand how my story *might just have a message beyond my family.*

With my favorite athlete.

Devin, like so many sons and daughters of Mary Kay Directors, grew up not really aware that his mom had a real job. All he knew was that I was very present in his day-to-day life during his growing-up years. Sometimes that was much to his chagrin!

I worked from home, and it didn't take very long for him to master the art of knowing precisely when I was otherwise occupied

> I came to understand how my story *might just have a message beyond my family.*

and might—in my distracted state—be more likely to grant a permission. Devin would wait until I was engrossed on a business call to appear at my office door. At a young age, he'd also perfected the annoying trick of balancing a baseball bat on the palm of his hand to get my immediate attention so he could ask me if it was okay if he rode his bike to so-and-so's house, or roasted marshmallows in the fireplace, or engaged in some other boisterous activity. One particular afternoon, he appeared balancing that baseball bat while I was in the midst of a phone call. Somehow

Devin on guitar.

the bat slipped out of his palm and crashed onto my head with a loud bang before bouncing onto my lap. As Devin tells it laughingly, "She never broke stride on her phone call. Without missing a beat, Mom removed the bat from her lap and handed it to me with a stern look. I already knew the answer to my question was No! and was pretty amazed that despite the knot appearing on her head, she continued with her conversation. The caller had no idea she'd just been seriously bopped on the head by a baseball bat. I made myself scarce for the rest of that day."

"I grew up watching my parents set goals and pursue their dreams. This was such a great lesson, but it's not something you can just turn on and off. Eventually, it simply becomes second nature. Of course, I never doubted myself or felt that the things I wanted to do might be impossible," he says, "because growing up surrounded by such a constant can-do attitude gave me the confidence to try new things." In Devin's pursuit of success, pursuing his own dreams, he accrued a bachelor's degree in English, a master's degree in accounting, became a licensed

> "Growing up surrounded by such a constant can-do attitude gave me the confidence to try new things."
> —DEVIN

CPA, and got his law degree. Today he has a private law practice and goes out of his way to use his financial and legal knowledge to help others, to give back, and to share many other subtle but extremely important life lessons. I sensed he also gleaned something else from the Mary Kay influence he grew up around: "My parents," he says, "raised me with the idea that every obstacle is an opportunity. You can get over, under, or around it if you just put your mind to it."

> "... every obstacle is an opportunity. You can get over, under, or around it if you just put your mind to it."
> — DEVIN

In the positions he has held with large corporations in real estate development, health care, insurance, and the legal profession, Devin tells me, he has noticed how much more gets done using the collegial and cooperative atmosphere Mary Kay fostered. "Everything comes down to a person making a decision," he says, "whether it's a young woman trying to decide if she wants to sign a Beauty Consultant agreement, or a seasoned judge who will decide whether or not to grant a certain motion."

Devin met his future wife Sandra when they were middle school band kids but they were well into high school before the two began dating. This was just as our twenty-fifth wedding anniversary was approaching and, to celebrate in style, Bruce had suggested we book a table at The Mansion on Turtle Creek, a

Devin being sworn in as an attorney by the Chief Justice.

perennial Dallas dining splurge. But before we could make the reservation for our usual party of three, Devin interrupted with, "may I invite Sandra?"

"I remember that evening how nervous I was," says Sandra, "but Bruce and Doretha not only put me at ease, they also asked me about my college plans and what career I might pursue. This dinner was the first of many with the Dinglers and the first of many conversations where I learned what I needed to know about setting goals, making a workable plan, and expecting the best for myself."

> This dinner was the first of many . . . where I learned what I needed to know about setting goals . . .

Sandra went on to study music and psychology at Bruce's alma mater. She was selected to Who's Who of American Colleges and Universities, chosen Texas Tech University Senior of the Year from among her graduating class of more than three thousand students, and graduated with a Bachelor of Arts, *summa cum laude*. After the birth of Brittany, Sandra developed a keen interest in architecture and interior design. She applied for part-time work at Laura Ashley and instead got hired on to their design team. Within the year, Sandra became the Lead Designer of Laura Ashley Home for North America. She completed her post-graduate work in architectural interior design at the world-famous Inch-

Devin escorts Sandra to the Presentation Ball of Gamma Phi Beta sorority.

bald School of Design in London, England. Thereafter, she received her diploma of distance tutoring at Oxford University. Currently, she tutors design students from around the world including the UK, France, Italy, Malta, New Zealand, Australia,

The Dinglers out to dinner in Connecticut.

Yemen, and Mauritius. Living her dream, she does it all just steps from Devin and Brittany in her converted-barn design studio.

"So much of who Brittany is today is Doretha upside down and sideways. Brittany will tell me of a plan she has and then ask me to think about it. She might say, 'It's nothing we have to decide right now. Nothing to say no to immediately. Let's talk about it later.'"

That really does sound like me! And you can imagine how I love hearing these observations. As you can tell, I am ex-tremely proud of my family but also gratified that the principles that guided me in my career have also benefited each of them as they pursue their own path in life.

Sandra, Devin, and Brittany.

Brittany on a visit to the zoo
with Bruce.

Visiting Brittany at preschool on
grandparent's day.

Brittany having a ball!

Tidbit

Ginger

13

The Power of the Stage—
A Forty-Year Journey

"We are what we repeatedly do."
—ARISTOTLE

My wish is that by the time you've arrived at this chapter, you will agree that I stayed true to the music selected as my "theme song"—"Accentuate the Positive" by Johnny Mercer and Harold Arlen. Each National Sales Director was to choose a theme song, so I selected this 1940s-era tune. It played every time I was introduced onto the Mary Kay stage and after speeches and countless other appearances. I chose to keep it as my song even after it started sounding a little dated. The reason? To use an old Texas phrase, I wanted to "dance with who brung ya." Besides, I always felt these lyrics and their sentiment had served me well, capturing my life and business philosophy. It sounds so simple—but choosing to "Accentuate the Positive" really did work for me.

> Choosing to "Accentuate the Positive" really did work for me.

I had started out so afraid of the stage and the limelight. When first asked to speak, I worried if I was the right voice and if I had the right message. Hearing this song all those times that it preceded me made it a familiar, almost comforting symbol that somehow allowed me to stay positive. Along with the song, it's interesting that the highlights of all those trips onstage are as vivid to me today as they were forty years ago. It seems to me as if the story of my life was, essentially, played out on that stage.

I had started out so afraid of the stage and the limelight.

With the blink of an eye, I can picture myself walking off the stage into Mary Kay's outstretched arms and her encouraging words that gave me the strength to continue to the next, and the next, and the next time. I can clearly recall squinting as I tried to spot the one person I knew in the audience when I went onstage for my Sales Director debut. She was seated in the back row of the Fairmont Hotel ballroom. (Both our husbands were on the golf course, oblivious as we all were to the significance of this giant step I was taking.) And the year I became a National Sales Director, that same friend—my first offspring Sales Director—ascended for the first time to the top Sales Director spot. So many times, I would look out and see the pride in their eyes when my family listened from the front row. And it was even more gratifying when they joined me onstage as an Independent National Sales Director and when I debuted as an Emeritus. I

I would look out and see the pride in their eyes when my family listened from the front row

shared with those Mary Kay audiences all my major life milestones: our son going to first grade and all the years in between, until suddenly he was bound for college, getting married, becoming a father, and so on. I recall all those happy times when Mary Kay Ash stood on stage to hug and congratulate us for yet another achievement. There was such pride on that stage when our Area was recognized for new achievements—like the year four of the top five Directors in our Seminar were Dingler Area offspring, or when we broke records for monthly commissions or reaching double-digit millions in career earnings. There was a tremendous feeling of accomplishment experienced during each of the nineteen times National Sales Directors debuted from our National Area. I could go on and on naming these momentous occasions.

There were also sobering times, those moments when we cried together or gathered strength from each other. I've already written about the year of Mary Kay's 1996 stroke, and when we first learned that Mary Kay would never again be with us onstage or in her office at headquarters in Dallas (a place that has been left intact for fifteen years now). Then it was the very year I made my march to No. 1 when our nation had to come to grips with the horrific reality of the

> There was a tremendous feeling of accomplishment experienced during each of the nineteen times National Sales Directors debuted from our National Area.

attacks of September 11, 2001, a time we all felt vulnerable. We suffered a personal loss just a few months later that same year, on November 22, when the Mary Kay world had to grapple with the death of Mary Kay on a somber Thanksgiving Day, her favorite holiday. Each of us would handle her loss individually and collectively—and, more important, we'd be called upon that year and beyond to draw strength from her legacy, assume her mantle of sales force leadership, and continue to move forward for all those who would never know her personally.

I still remember the lump in my throat as I stood in the wings waiting that January. I was to speak at the first Mary Kay sales force gathering following both of these significant historical events. I used to think I knew what butterflies felt like, but that day I felt the tremendous weight of responsibility and hoped I could carry it. I knew the words I chose would be extremely important to set the tone for our leaders at Mary Kay. While each of us would have to find the strength to carry on and continue to motivate others, some of us would need to find that strength and talk about what it felt like. We wouldn't have those affectionate nudges we'd always had from Mary Kay Ash, an enormously influential woman who had changed our lives by believing in us so deeply. As I walked up the long flight of stairs toward the stage floor, I knew that now it was our turn. It was the time, we—her sisters, daughters, and friends— needed to be brave just like she was in the face of fear. I needed to use the power of that stage now more than ever. The words to one of Mary Kay's favorite Bible verses repeated themselves in my head: *What time I am afraid, I will think of thee.* (Psalm 56:3)

Upon Mary Kay's passing, I was interviewed by a Dallas newspaper. The following are excerpts from that article.

Doretha Dingler of Dallas, who worked with Mrs. Ash for more than 30 years, was among the legions whom Mary Kay mentored.

"She's a person who unleashed the talents of women," Mrs. Dingler said. "When she formed her company, women couldn't even sign their name to a bank loan. She's brought us up to where women own banks."

Mrs. Ash mentored her sales force in much the same way her mother had mentored her when Mary Kay was a child, Mrs. Dingler said.

"Mary Kay would just be there

LOSS OF A LEGEND

Mary Kay dies

Mary Kay Ash, who rode to the top of the cosmetics world with pink Cadillacs as sales incentives, died Thursday at her home in Dallas.

saying, 'You can do it, you can do it.' " she said.

"Mary Kay probably produced the first career women in the world," Mrs. Dingler said. "We were teachers, secretaries, nurses, whatever, but career women — no way."

It was clear to me that everyone in the arena that day, and everyone who would listen via tape around the world, would be called upon to gather a double dose of strength, both for our nation and for our company's founder. At the very turn of this new century, I suddenly knew how so many pioneers had probably felt as their long journey was coming to a close.

Yes, here I was on the threshold of retirement wanting nothing more than to send a clear message to all of my sister Nationals and Sales Directors. The message I hoped to convey to everyone from the Gen Yers to the pre–Baby Boomers, and all those in between, was that we now had the privilege to carry this great woman's legacy forward in the new century. Shouldering this responsibility fell to all of us who wanted to be certain Mary Kay ideals would continue to shine throughout the world. I knew long before that day that Mary Kay's ideals for business and for life are the right ones. On that day, I felt fully confident I was up to the task to breathe that belief into everyone listening.

> I finally fully understood that I was the right person of the right age and the right background to stand before this audience . . .

That same sense of being in the right place at the right time followed me onstage as I made my final Seminar address. After countless Seminar speeches, going back to my first one in 1969, I had come to more fully understand what we call the power of the stage. On that momentous day, as I was about to make that walk leading to my final time at the podium, an almost palpable silence pierced my consciousness. There was a calm—both inside and out. Instead of feeling my blood pressure racing, I had a feeling of peace. I finally fully understood that I was the right person of the right age and with the right background to stand before this audience and leave them with a meaningful message at this significant time in our history. I could hear the audience and feel their applause as the announcer's crisp voice read the accolades of my career. For just a brief moment, I had a flashback and felt the full measure of the immense distance that separated this final day from my first day onstage thirty-three years earlier. What a contrast between the me who'd so tentatively tiptoed to the stage and grasped the microphone like a life raft in 1969 and this twenty-first-century, modern, successful woman striding confidently to the stage—even dancing a few steps—that one last time. I was a self-made woman, shaped by the power of Mary Kay's belief in me.

> What a contrast between the me who'd so tentatively tiptoed to the stage . . . in 1969 . . .

Everything had altered so dramatically—the landscape for women, the trajectory of our families, the expectations of our communities, and the promise of our futures. Our own self-image, not to mention our poise and grace, were forces to be reckoned with. That day I stood quietly aware of every nuance as I waited in the darkened little alcove at the top of the steps to go to the podium one final time. It was there I realized that this stage was now the place where I felt most comfortable. This stage had become like home for me. It was where I was supposed to be. I could look out into the audience and see the lives that had changed. I could believe, finally, all the women who had told me I was responsible for making a difference, all the letters I had received from women all over the world who said they could relate to my story,

> I was a self-made woman, shaped by the power of Mary Kay's belief in me.

> I could believe, finally, all the women who had told me I was responsible for making a difference.

Taken at our last Seminar with Sandra and Devin.

all those who'd thanked me for showing them how to achieve their dreams, who appreciated my sharing the fears and failures of my journey with them and all the husbands and families who had thanked me for altering their stories for the better. For someone like me, this was a heady feeling. It was a little intoxicating to come to a personal realization that maybe I had indeed left behind something valuable, that in sharing a little piece of myself in each of those trips to the podium, in classes and individually with so many women over the years, I had been doing exactly what Mary Kay had asked of her leaders. I knew that for the rest of my life, I would never forget all those faces, all the feelings I had been privileged to be a part of. It is a wonderful sense of accomplishment to reach a point in your life when you know you mattered, that you had achieved the vision to see the things that needed doing and the ability to do them. I, the fifth woman to become a National Sales Director and only one of

> It is a wonderful sense of accomplishment to reach a point in your life when you know you mattered.

five women to ever reign as the No. 1 National Sales Director worldwide, was now passing that proverbial baton. I had made the history books, but far more important was that I'd learned to believe that I deserved to have reached the top and to have worn the queen's crown. I was physically drained from the journey, yet my heart was filled to the brim.

That feeling has remained with me even after my retirement, as I have experienced an appreciation only time can bestow upon us. I've also come to the realization that we never really retire emotionally from a career we loved so much. Physically, yes, but when you have bettered yourself, had such a life-changing experience, when you are mentored by a world-class hero, and when you work with so many thousands of women and your opinions matter to the professionals at a global corporation, these things never leave you. For all of us fortunate enough to share the history of a legendary company, we will always be part of it. The corporation Mary Kay founded has taken pains to assure us that we still matter to the company after we retire. This was brought home to me when

Bruce and I exercised the option to travel with the National Sales Directors on any three trips of our choosing during our first five years of retirement. We eventually opted for a wonderful trip to St. Petersburg, Russia, on a glorious private yacht

With the captain on our trip to St. Petersburg, Russia, via Copenhagen and Stockholm.

on which the only passengers were the Mary Kay group. Three years after I retired I was accorded the same first-class privileges on

that cruise I had enjoyed as the No. 1 National Sales Director. The status this accords those of us who were accustomed to the Mary Kay limelight is a wonderful way to remain connected and to move gently and gracefully into retirement. One more thing about this perk that I especially appreciated was that when the usual Mary Kay recognition was handed out in the meetings aboard that luxurious ship, my record earnings were included and applauded. What a wonderful thing they did to Make Me Feel Important (MMFI) in the true spirit of Mary Kay Ash. Oh my goodness, did it feel good on that trip for those few minutes of recognition to be in the limelight again! I found it to be quite energizing.

I said early on in writing this book that I felt I could start out today and do as well, if not better, than I had done previously. Just this year, I was asked to share my insight with a young Mary Kay Sales Director whose uncle is a family friend; I realized that even though the times and the products are very different, the Mary Kay principles by which I succeeded haven't changed at all. The secrets to success remain very much the same in a time and place that are so markedly different from my own. And my advice to this young, new Sales Director was not that different from what I'd taught the women in my Area for more than a quarter of a century.

> . . . between your ears lies a vast promised land of opportunity waiting to be unleashed.

Like Mary Kay always told us, success in this business is "between the ears." The pure psychology of *In Pink* is that between your ears lies a vast promised land of opportunity waiting to be unleashed. It takes the right opportunity for sure. It also takes an impeccable work ethic and strong values. And it asks that you develop strengths, techniques, and tactics that are yours alone. Between your years from the start to the finish of your career lies the fertile area where almost any woman is able to bloom where she is planted. The two Greenvilles of my life in Texas and South Carolina and the time we spent working in Arizona, Florida, and elsewhere have shown me that it's not about geography or topography. It's all about your commitment.

For me, it was also never just about selling lipstick. It was about making a difference, seeing all the opportunities that women are fully capable of creating for themselves once they open their minds to seizing the opportunity and doing it. It was about becoming the kind of role model and mentor who can take insecure women by the hand and lead them where they need to go—and the kind of leader who can take them to a certain point, then step back and watch them soar.

> For me it was also never just about selling lipstick.

Oh yes, it is true that in retirement you do wake up one morning with this feeling that there's something you've forgotten, something surely you just have to do. After all those years of going and doing, traveling, influencing so many people, of teaching and speaking and interfacing in thousands of lives, I must admit I spent a few months searching for the right pace—seeking that proper blueprint for retirement. Then I discovered, after all that fruitless searching, there is none. Coming off of a career

> I spent a few months searching for the right pace—seeking that proper blueprint for retirement. Then I discovered, after all that fruitless searching, there is none.

whose success track was spelled out in very clear detail and whose career ladder was the same for everyone—it's no wonder I guess that I just halfway assumed there had to be some sort of model for retirement. What I found is that it doesn't exist. There is no one model for success, and certainly not one for sitting back and basking in that success.

But what I've also found is that the same things that make one successful in a business can easily be applied to the business of retirement. What made for a successful family and marriage in one's career are still the key ingredient after the curtain is drawn across the stage.

Even in retirement, "Accentuate the Positive" remains my theme song. Today, when I hear of an acquaintance that can't be approved for a needed surgery because he's not able to wade through the maze of forms and requirements, I certainly can and will help him. When I can coach my dental hygienist as to what her next Mary Kay career move should be, I most definitely will exert a positive influence on her doubts. If it takes repeated trial and error to get our medical prescription regimen right, or our lab results where they should be, I will try and try to get that right. I will listen intently when my newly retired friend confides she feels that a giant door has been slammed in her face. I will try to show her a way to the same kind of peace I have found. I will politely demur, however, when asked to get involved in the decisions of a corporate structure in which I am no longer a significant stakeholder. When I see something not working properly, or someone not treated right, it is a given I will do my best to see that the situation is remedied. I know the ropes, I know the course, and I am never afraid to navigate it.

> As I think of the odds of repeating my success in today's world, I am fully confident it could be done.

Figuring out what drives people, as I did for all those many years, is a learned skill. The ability to read people is something that gets better with practice. And make no mistake: I continue to practice all that I learned.

As I think of the odds of repeating my success in today's world, I am fully confident it could be done. Springboarding off a dazzling company and personal website would be a piece of cake. All the conveniences of the thoroughly modern Mary Kay would be a walk in the park for someone like me who once had to bake the display trays in my oven to sanitize them after every class, or mix the foundation shades to match certain skin types. To anyone who once answered the "Mary Kay Who?" question so many thousands of times, explaining or proving the worth of a second look at this legend and her legacy would be so simple in a time when her ideals

Introducing Brittany to the power of the stage.

are so respected. There are still so many millions of women who have what's needed to sell this fine product: they have skin. And like Mary Kay, if I were to pursue my business anew today, I'd still consider everyone with skin to be within my reach and on my radar! I would continue to find millions of fine and worthy women who have a need for the opportunity inherent in a marketing plan that sees the potential between the ears of any woman, from any background.

> In this age of 24/7 everything, I truly believe that I could parlay a Mary Kay business into double what I did my last several years—and maybe in half the time.

In this age of 24/7 everything, I truly believe that I could parlay a Mary Kay business into double what I did my last several years—

and maybe in half the time. If I was on target for a million a year in commissions at the turn of this century, today I believe I'd be gunning for two. There is no reason I couldn't. How about you? The clock is ticking off those precious seconds. You needn't waste one of them. Hum a few bars of "Accentuate the Positive" with me before you go out and soar.

The stage is set. All eyes are on you now.

At the podium
Embracing the power of the stage

Mary Kay

Excerpts from tributes made to Mary Kay Ash upon her death in November 2001

TRIBUTES

Laura Bush, First Lady
"Mary Kay is someone I have always admired. I believe that America's greatness is due in large part to courageous people like Mary Kay who have never been afraid to stand up for what is right."

Doretha Dingler, Mary Kay Executive National Sales Director
"Mary Kay asked that we take our families along on this journey. She knew that if we mold ourselves into positive, inspiring role models for our families, they would have a head start on living their own journey successfully."

"Mary Kay blazed the trail in the area of economic liberation for women! She has empowered women and enabled them to build a better life for themselves and their families. Mary Kay will go down in history as one of the greatest female humanitarians and visionaries of our time."

Zig Ziglar, Motivational Speaker
"Mary Kay is an outstanding person in all areas: a hardworking astute, self-made, warm and friendly human being who goes above and beyond the call of duty to spread the good word about life, love, and hope, which is so badly needed in America today. Her own personal success is founded on an intense desire to help other people and the willingness to start early and work late to accomplish her objectives."

Fannie Flagg, author of *Fried Green Tomatoes*
"Mary Kay is my heroine. She cares so much for women, and she meant so much to my mother and so much to my mother's friends who changed their lives in Alabama."

Roger Staubach, Former Quarterback, Dallas Cowboys
"Mary Kay eloquently reminds us the only way to successfully manage all areas of our lives is to have our values and priorities in place."

Rev. Dr. Robert Schuller, Crystal Cathedral, Garden Grove, CA
"Mary Kay Ash has set an example of how our free enterprise system works that is thrilling indeed. Her life is a glowing testimony of a person who sets goals, follows them through with determination, uses innovative methods in a creative manner, but at the same time is motivated by a genuine desire to help people achieve unusual success."

Acknowledgments

I want to acknowledge the following people who have made valuable contributions to my life and career.

First and foremost to my very best friend and husband, Bruce, who has been by my side loving and supporting me throughout this journey; his priceless contribution made this book possible.

To my son, Devin, who has worked very closely and diligently with me in writing this book and without whose expertise this book would not have been completed. To his wife, Sandra, and our granddaughter, Brittany, who have been very supportive of this endeavor.

My parents, George and Doris (both deceased), sisters Glenda and Georgina, and brother, George, who have been so much a part of who I am today; not to mention my extended family, many of whom are still a part of my life.

I wish to thank Mary Kay, my mentor, without whom hundreds of thousands of women worldwide would have never had the opportunity that empowered us to make a difference in the lives of so many people; Richard, her son, and his son, Ryan, who continue to keep Mary Kay's dream alive. To David Holl, CEO, who was chosen by the Mary Kay family as the person to lead this company not only in the United States but worldwide and who has done and continues to do an outstanding job.

Mary Kay's legacy, the Mary Kay Ash Charitable Foundation, is helping to continue to make a difference through cancer research, women's shelters, and many other important women's issues, as well as the Mary Kay Museum managed by Jennifer Cook and staff. We must never forget the contribution Mary Kay's assistant, Erma Thomson, made in helping to support all of Mary Kay's endeavors. Of course to Mary Kay's U.S. President, Darrell Overcash, who is doing a great job.

The nineteen National Sales Directors and 1st line NSDs at the time of my retirement from whom I received enormous support: Joan Chadbourn, Sharon Parris, Nan Stroud, Anita Tripp-Brewton, Cheryl Warfield, and Barbara Sunden, who currently is the No. 1 NSD in Mary Kay. Barbara has taken the number one position to an all new record-breaking level, giving me credit as her mentor—an honor of which I am extremely proud. A very special thank you to the tens of thousands of NSDs, Directors, and Consultants from the Dingler Area in multiple countries around the world for your tremendous contribution to the success of our Area.

A special thank-you to my fellow original Top 10 Nationals with whom I had the privilege of traveling with Mary Kay to see the world through her eyes, and the many other Emeritus Nationals with whom I have remained friends throughout the years.

A special thank-you to my friend and assistant for over twenty plus years, Paula Funderburk, whose tremendous support both personally and professionally have made it possible for me to make this journey.

To worldwide motivational speaker Zig Ziglar, with whom I

had the opportunity to work in the early days of my Mary Kay career, and who was gracious enough to be a part of this book.

To Yvonne Pendleton whose contribution to *In Pink* was enormous, including countless hours spent collaborating on this book, and to Whitney MacKay for her invaluable research.

To Candace Johnson and Carol Rosenberg, whose invaluable editorial expertise ensured that *In Pink* was produced at the highest level of literary excellence; and to Gary Rosenberg, whose skillful interior and cover design brought the book to life.

To Dr. Casey Caldwell of the Mayo Clinic, Dr. Arthur Shannon (retired), and Dr. Phillip Aronoff, whose medical expertise has been invaluable in managing family medical issues. They are all good friends as well.

To our many friends throughout the years who have offered their friendship, Bob and Pam Weems (Bob was responsible for transferring us to South Carolina), Jackie and Evelyn Martin, George and Dot Warren, Sid and Hilda Collier (Pam, Evelyn, Dot, and Hilda hosted my very first Mary Kay classes), Harold and Peggy Larison, Dr. Merwyn and Polly Pickle, Jerry and Sandra Holland, John and Carla Owens (Carla keeps us occasionally updated on Athens events), Jimmy Mitchell (who provided my mother's 1936 senior yearbook picture for this book), and so many others who we enjoy seeing when we visit Athens for special events.

To my Athens, Texas, classmates: Damon Douglas, our class president, who has always planned our class reunions; Dr. George Lowe, valedictorian, who we keep in touch with; my fellow honor students; and the many other classmates from first through twelfth grade (names too numerous to mention).

A special thank you to Yale Goldberg, a friend whose legal expertise has been invaluable to us over many years. Also to Glen Antle, for being a trusted and great friend for forty plus years. To our estate planner, Hope Leibsohn, whose expert legal and financial advice has been an immense help to us over the years. To CPA Charles Rives, CFP Cynthia Romognolo, and Michelle Maxcy, whose expertise has been greatly appreciated.

There are so many others both personally and professionally who have offered friendship and support over the years who possibly have unintentionally not been mentioned. Please forgive my oversight. Special efforts have been made to identify the subject of each story where permission was granted.

I want to acknowledge and thank those who are carrying Mary Kay's dream to women around the world: KK Chua, Asia Pacific Regional President; Tara Eustace, European Regional President; Pepe Smeke, Latin America Regional President; and to Ray Patrick, Mary Kay Canada, for all the help he gave me working with the thousands of Consultants, Directors, and National Sales Directors from the Dingler Area in Canada.

Finally I want to acknowledge the many women I'll never meet, those who'll assume Mary Kay's leadership mantle and take her vision to new heights across the world. I'll be watching you!

About the Author

Doretha Dingler is an Elite Executive Independent National Sales Director Emeritus of Mary Kay, Inc. Joining the company shortly after it was founded by Mary Kay Ash in the early sixties, Doretha worked closely with Mary Kay from the company's early years until her passing in 2001 and still considers her the most significant role model for women in business today. After retiring from a nearly forty-year career, Doretha still devotes time to writing, teaching, and encouraging others to continue Mary Kay's priceless legacy of empowering women.

Through this book, Doretha seeks to educate and inspire women around the world, in developed and developing countries, with practical tips of running a woman-owned business combined with timeless principles of personal and people management.

A special plaque is being displayed in Mary Kay world headquarters recognizing the seven NSDs in the fifty-year history of this multi-billion dollar company who have reached the pinnacle of the sales force by attaining the coveted No. 1 position in commissions nationally. Upon her retirement, Doretha was the fifth NSD to have earned this prestigious title.

Yvonne Pendleton, whose contribution to *In Pink* has been invaluable, is an award-winning journalist whose words helped tell the Mary Kay story and shape the company profile from the time it first became a billion-dollar corporation until today. Her many contributions, published worldwide in Chinese, Russian, and Spanish, include *Wall Street Journal* and *New York Times* bestsellers.

The portrait on the front cover is one of the original oil paintings displayed in the Mary Kay Hall of Fame.

The bell on the front cover and throughout the book was the symbol for the Dingler Area. They were referred to as the "Dingler Belles" for almost forty years.